UNLEASH **YOUR BS** (BEST SELF)

"This is not a typical business book. It has more twists and turns than a daytime soap opera. Jeff Black is a dear friend, who can make a world of difference in your professional career."

—**Eileen Fulton**—Actress
Starring as "Lisa" on CBS-TV's *As the World Turns*
Procter & Gamble Productions

"*Unleash your BS* captures the essence of Jeff's teaching and storytelling in a lighthearted way! It is a great business story that brings to life the corporate environment in moments of crisis, while providing simple to digest tactics to improve one's personal brand. This is a book that professionals will enjoy reading ... helping them become self-aware of their own style and improving their communication and influencing skills."

—**Lilkar Molina**
MBA, Senior Engineer—Procter & Gamble
Executive Board of Directors—Hispanic Chamber Cincinnati USA

"*Unleash Your BS* is Jeff Black at his very best ... doing what he loves to do ... in his own unique and very 'real' way. He will make a positive difference for his readers—just as he has (and does!) for me."

—**Paula Harper Bethea**
Executive Director—South Carolina Education Lottery
Former Chair—United Way of America

"This is a dynamic and fun manual for staging effective communications! Each act in this book presents a practical model for real world business environments!"

—**Dr. Shue-Jane Thompson**
Director, Performance Excellence—Lockheed Martin Corporation

"I first met Jeff Black when he was working in the mailroom at Aaron Spelling Productions. I immediately noticed that he possessed a unique presence, so I quickly hired him into Business Affairs where he was a true partner. Since that time, we've stayed in touch and I am now thrilled to be endorsing his book. We share the same values and integrity and know the importance of passing on to others what we've learned."

—Beth Whelpley
Vice President, Business Affairs—NBC Universal

"Regardless of your experience as a communicator, Jeff Black's *Unleash Your BS* should be on your "must read" list. The concepts are conveyed through stories that are fun to read, yet packed with important lessons on how to improve your communications, enhance your influencing skills and be your "best self."

—Kimberly Admire
Former Vice President, Culture, Diversity and Equal Opportunity Programs, Lockheed Martin Corporation

UNLEASH YOUR BS (BEST SELF)

PUT YOUR EXECUTIVE PRESENCE TO THE TEST

JEFF BLACK

—— WITH ——

CAROL HAMILTON & KIMBERLY FAITH MADDEN

NEW YORK

UNLEASH **YOUR BS** (BEST SELF)
PUT YOUR EXECUTIVE PRESENCE TO THE TEST

Published in New York, New York, by Morgan James Publishing. Morgan James and The Entrepreneurial Publisher are trademarks of Morgan James, LLC. www.MorganJamesPublishing.com

The Morgan James Speakers Group can bring authors to your live event. For more information or to book an event visit The Morgan James Speakers Group at www.TheMorganJamesSpeakersGroup.com.

This book is a work of fiction. Names, characters, places, and incidents either are products of the author's imagination or are used fictitiously. Any resemblance to actual events or locales or persons, living or dead, is entirely coincidental.

For information, address Black Sheep, P.O. Box 65, Manning, SC 29102.

ISBN 978-1-63047-357-0 paperback
ISBN 978-1-63047-358-7 eBook
ISBN 978-1-63047-359-4 hardcover
Library of Congress Control Number: 2014945086

A **free** eBook edition is available with the purchase of this print book.

CLEARLY PRINT YOUR NAME ABOVE IN UPPER CASE

Instructions to claim your free eBook edition:
1. Download the BitLit app for Android or iOS
2. Write your name in **UPPER CASE** on the line
3. Use the BitLit app to submit a photo
4. Download your eBook to any device

Cover Design by:
Rachel Lopez
www.r2cdesign.com

Interior Design by:
Bonnie Bushman
bonnie@caboodlegraphics.com

In an effort to support local communities, raise awareness and funds, Morgan James Publishing donates a percentage of all book sales for the life of each book to Habitat for Humanity Peninsula and Greater Williamsburg.

Get involved today, visit
www.MorganJamesBuilds.com

Habitat for Humanity®
Peninsula and Greater Williamsburg
Building Partner

DEDICATION

Since I "preach" on the Power of Three (three messages, three tough questions, three points per slide), here are my dedications:

1. To my wife, Stephanie, and children, Liz and John Landon, who don't see much of me but always welcome me home with great love. I am so grateful to them for allowing me to pursue my passion. I know it's difficult having a spouse and a father who spends more time with flight attendants than his own family. (No, John Landon, you're not getting a Range Rover. This book won't generate enough money for that.)
2. For my parents who struggle with cancer, and to my thirty-year-old sister who died from it...you have all shown me steadfast courage and amazing grace. Special thanks to my dad: It's because of him that my communication consulting company, Black Sheep, was born. I just couldn't sell Buick

LeSabres at his GM dealership. ("Dad, what's the difference between a V-6 and a V-8?")

3. And in memory of Annie Gibson who taught me the most important characteristic of leadership...never give up. In 1949, just ten miles from my home, she signed a petition asking for separate but equal opportunities for the children in her community. That petition was the origins of the landmark school desegregation case in 1953, *Brown vs. The Board of Education*. This very private woman shared her "story" with me, and I am a better person for it.

—**Jeffrey T. Black**, the Black Sheep

TABLE OF CONTENTS

To be a great communicator, you have to have some acting skills.
—Jeff Black

PREFACE

By Jeff Black

I write this Preface, somewhere over the Atlantic Ocean, heading back to the U.S. after delivering my three-day executive presence program in Krakow, Poland. Much of my life is spent traveling from one program to the next, heading to a group of twelve participants, an audience of hundreds, or a one-on-one coaching session with a client. After eighteen years and twenty countries, I still love every single minute of it. (Well, except the part about delayed flights and lost luggage. One time, I borrowed a sports coat to wear from a waiter at a hotel restaurant in Stamford, CT.)

Back to Poland for a moment...the participants were from an international corporation. I was hired to help them with their executive presence, overall communication and presentation skills, and perhaps most importantly, their personal brands. One of the participants said to me: "Jeff, certainly you believe that communication skills are based primarily on culture. For example, your idea of using Powerful Opening

Words (POW), to start a presentation or meeting doesn't work in some places, right?" I paused, quickly thought back to my global work, and said, "It works in every country I visit. How you deliver the message might vary, but the key ingredients never change—strong openings, compelling messages, and good stories."

Throughout this book, you'll find real-world stories woven into the experiences of our characters, along with tangible tools that demonstrate how you can authentically sell your brand in a crowded marketplace. The competition has never been greater in this twenty-four/seven world in which we live. Just doing a good job is usually not enough to advance in an organization. You have to "lead and be heard." You have to think about your communication skills, your ability to manage an audience, your social interactions, your professional appearance, and your visibility. Those who do are on a faster track, I promise. One of my clients said to me recently: "I've been so busy selling my company's brand that I forgot to sell my own." This is an important lesson for us to learn.

Over the years, I've spoken to thousands of people, many of them at large companies: GE, American Airlines, Procter & Gamble, NBC Universal, Bank of America, and M&M Mars, just to name a few. I realize I have been incredibly fortunate in my career, especially when I think back to how and when it all started. It's doubtful my first presentation was my best, but as I tell my audiences, practice does make all of us better. It would be wrong of me not to acknowledge one client in particular—GE. An executive saw my work and gave me an opportunity. All these years later, this company remains my largest client, and I have developed many wonderful friendships within this organization over the years.

I often tell participants, "I know this seems like a large amount of time out of the office, but your company has just given you a G&O. No, this has nothing to do with Goals and Objectives. Your company leaders think enough of you that they are investing in your brand. G&O stands for what you are being given here—a Gift and an Opportunity." Upon reflection, I believe I'm the one who has been given the G&O. Thank you for buying this book, but more importantly, thank you for letting me share with you what I know it takes to get ahead. You'll find the tips and strategies easy to implement, without investing a great amount of time—something that is precious to both you and your career. Be prepared to strengthen your executive presence, your communication skills, and your brand. Go forth and *Unleash Your BS!*

THE CAST

Black Sheep
JT—Executive Presence Consultant

Decision-Makers

Massive Industries	Cascade Corporation
Tom Harris—CEO	Yuan Luo—CEO
Kelly—Senior Vice President of HR	

Participants

Massive Industries	Cascade Corporation
Andrei—Director of Operations	David—Director of Manufacturing
Ron—Director of Purchasing	Al—Plant Manager
Laleh—Regional Director of Training	Ajay—Director of Engineering
Ann—Director of IT	Mizuki—HR Administrator

CHARACTER DESCRIPTIONS

Andrei, fluent in several languages and an engineer with an Ivy-league degree, inhabited an island of self-satisfaction. His education and prior career in the military had catapulted him to Director of Operations at Massive not long before the merger. Thus, he had surpassed the stages wherein a great leader acquires humility. As a result, Andrei's success had left him few proponents and no friends.

Ron was often referred to as a "character" around Massive. His three-word resume read: brilliant—direct—sarcastic. He'd had enough victories to attain the position Director of Purchasing, yet in the decade since, all of his promotions were merely lateral moves. With time and opportunities racing by, both his frustration and his cynicism grew daily.

Laleh, a bright, well educated, and popular young manager, had earned her title, Regional Director of Training & Leadership Development at Massive. Her good looks and charm, as well as her spot-on instincts regarding human behavior, led her up the corporate ladder quickly. The merger had spurred a momentary concern about her future, but then a recruiter called with multiple job offers, and she'd slept soundly ever since.

Ann, the Massive Director of IT, had spent her career battling for recognition in her male-dominated field. Her reputation as a fierce competitor had won her accolades and financial abundance, as well as scathing criticism and a reputation for being "a cold fish," "uptight," and worse. In performance reviews, Ann had often been told she needed to soften her personality in order to advance.

David, the Director of Manufacturing for Cascade, had spent the majority of his professional life at Cascade, and he had dreaded the merger with the behemoth Massive from the first rumblings of it. Since the announcement, he'd been diligently defending employees from layoffs and being poached.

Al, a Plant Manager, had been with Cascade his entire career, as had his father and grandfather. The family was solid, New England stock that all lived on the same block, attended the same church, and drank at the same corner bar on Friday night. Al had surpassed everyone's expectations by becoming plant manager, so he felt no need to prove anything. Still, he couldn't help but wonder if retirement, sooner rather than later, was in his cards.

Ajay had accepted his position as Director of Engineering for Cascade two years prior, long before the merger was revealed. In his excitement about his promotion, he'd managed to convince his reluctant wife, children, and parents that the family would thrive in America. Now he was second-guessing that decision.

Mizuki, the youngest of the group, had found herself in a state of perpetual confusion. She had accepted a new position with Cascade less than a year before only to hear the rumor she should expect to be laid off in the merger; then suddenly she was transferred to the US, where upon arrival, she received a bewildering directive from a distasteful Senior VP at Massive regarding this training. She couldn't help but wonder if she should pursue a more stable situation.

Act 1: Scene I

A TALE OF TWO COMPANIES

T he audience sat in thick silence as the paperwork was passed from Tom Harris, CEO of Massive Industries to Yuan Luo, CEO of Cascade Corporation. Eight months of labored negotiations led to this single moment…this last dotted line, and too much was riding on the merger for anyone to risk breathing.

Slowly picking up a pen, Yuan allowed himself an extra moment in the spotlight. His retirement began with this final act on behalf of Cascade, and he felt a wave of nostalgia as he poised his hand to sign himself out.

Cascade Corporation was an international manufacturer that employed thousands. Yuan had been at the helm for the past twenty years and was responsible for the company's profound growth. Today, Cascade was becoming a subsidiary of Massive Industries, a conglomerate five times its size. Between them, the two companies had an impressive one hundred thirty years of service. However, as every critic had already pointed out, merging corporate cultures wasn't going to be easy, and in the end, no one was sure how this giant hybrid would work out.

Yuan looked over at Tom one last time and then completed his trademark signature. Instantly, the stockholders erupted into thunderous applause, the lawyers exhaled, and the management on both sides felt chills race down their spines.

Kelly entered Tom's office wearing her first smile since the announcement of the merger. "He's available," she announced as she dropped onto the nearest chair. Noting Tom's puzzled expression, she explained, "JT, the executive branding expert I mentioned to you. He just called to say he's ready to begin hosting executive presence programs for all of our managers at his retreat center."

Leaning back in his chair, Tom looked at the ceiling as if scanning his brain for information. Coming up dry, he turned to Kelly, "Remind me again what this guy's story is."

"Sure," Kelly answered, sitting up. "JT is the guy I saw several years ago. He's…" Kelly paused, trying to find the words to explain this unique man who had since become a dear friend, "…I guess the best way to describe him is engaging—and *certainly* entertaining—but underneath his light-hearted delivery is a very real depth of expertise on this topic."

Kelly clearly remembered the first time she'd seen JT present.

Walking to the front of the room, JT's tailored appearance and confident stride could easily have led someone to assume he was one of the leaders from the audience. But JT quickly set himself apart when he posed the question, "How many of you came here expecting a lot of depth, substance, and expertise on this career-changing topic, executive presence?" As several hands went up in the air, he'd proclaimed, "Those of you expecting a lot of depth all need to lower your expectations because I don't have very much. But I do have style."

Smiling, Kelly looked up to see Tom waiting for the rest of her story.

"The program begins with a pre-course survey on executive presence that gets everyone thinking about the subject.[1] The course itself is based on an interactive quiz regarding specific communication tools and incorporates multiple practice sessions with feedback for each participant," she explained.

Kelly paused, searching for a way to convey how powerful she felt this program was. "His techniques are deceptively simple, and yet exponentially enhance anyone's executive presence. Afterwards, everyone in the room finds him- or herself far more confident in building and giving presentations, networking, and even delivering difficult news."

Unconsciously scratching her head as she recalled the transformations she'd seen and personally experienced, she added, "This program is the best I've seen, and I've been in this business for a long time. As for his off-site location, it's a great fit for team-building."

"And how exactly do you see this playing into our situation?" Tom inquired.

"Well, we have two teams of leadership merging where there's only room for one. By putting each executive through a session of this program and observing who soars, we'll get to pick the cream of the crop for our new team, which serves us tremendously." Tom nodded in agreement but remained solemn, knowing soon they'd be forced to relinquish a lot of very talented people.

---

1   Scan this QR code to take the Black Sheep Executive Presence
    pre-course survey.

In an effort to lighten Tom's load, Kelly added, "As a side benefit, we'll also be giving each of them the opportunity to develop their professional skills, and that's something they'll have…wherever they end up working."

Recognizing that this program had promise, Tom stood up and instructed Kelly to proceed. Then locking eyes, he reminded her, "There's a lot at stake."

"Yes, there certainly is." Kelly quietly agreed as she left Tom's office.

Act 1: Scene II

THE PARTICIPANTS ARRIVE

The setting chosen for their training surprised the program participants. Rather than being pent up in a company conference room, they were sent off-site to a private oceanfront retreat designed to help attendees unwind. Upon arrival they were each given a tour and then instructed to do their utmost to unplug during the training. The next morning, they found water pitchers and note pads laid out on the expansive dining table in the Great Room.

Andrei arrived first and settled in to the right of the head of the table. Soon after, Ron entered the room, thus confirming what Andrei had already suspected—this "training" was useless to him. None of these attendees, even those from Massive, would have the power to further his career. Sighing at this obvious waste of his time, he returned to his computer.

Though no one had told Ron directly, he was convinced this training would determine his future. Nervously, he poured his third cup of coffee and silently wondered if his glass ceiling was made of cement. Neither of them looked at each other as he placed himself several chairs down from Andrei.

Laleh entered the room laughing into her phone and walking at the pace of youth. As a member of the training and learning team, it in was in her job description to attend a variety of training sessions and she loved every minute of it. Without hanging up, she nodded politely to her silent coworkers, set her things down at the far end of the table, and then stepped to the window to watch a pelican hunt for its breakfast.

The room was still quiet when Ann's purposeful footsteps announced her arrival. Known for getting results from her team, Ann had thought her leadership style was appreciated until she'd received the order to attend this training. Few things annoyed her more than unnecessary training, but Ann was far too politically correct to ever have spoken her frustration out loud. Primly, she seated herself next to Andrei, straightened the pen and pad on the table in front of her, and then folded her arms tightly across her chest.

As the Massive managers busied themselves, the door blew open, rattling in its hinges. Startled, all heads turned toward the noise where they discovered a man the size of a Grizzly bear filling the threshold.

David paused long enough in the doorway to assess the room and its occupants. Satisfied there was no imminent danger, he directed his Cascade colleagues to the left side of the table.

Tensions had run high between the management teams of the merging companies, as it was clear there wasn't room for everyone from both corporations. Taking them out for a private breakfast, David had done all he could to assure his fellow Cascadians their positions would not be filled by Mass-holes (as they'd all enjoyed calling them). He intentionally positioned himself to sit directly across from Andrei, a man David had heard enough about to be wary of, though the two had never met. Andrei closed his computer and observed David's every move. Andrei's research had revealed David to be the only serious threat to his ambitions, so he saw today as an opportunity to establish his place as leader of the pack.

Al sat down on David's left, and all he could hear was the voice in his head asking if it was time to retire. Over and over, he pictured his Lazy Boy and wondered if he really wanted to deal with all this change. He shook his head and looked down at his hands, avoiding any eye contact with the Mass-holes.

Ajay sat down with a smile planted on his face to cover his horror at the situation. It had been such a short time since he'd tied his future to Cascade. Now, he was sitting in a room waiting to participate in a battle that would determine whether or not he kept his work visa. He had nodded his greeting to each of the Massive managers rather than shaking their hands, so no one would notice his sweaty palms.

Mizuki sat in her chair with wide eyes, nervously shaking her foot. For the past year, her career had taken her on a dizzying roller coaster ride. She had no idea what to expect from this training, much less the merger, her orders…it was all so surreal—at this point, she did little but worry about what might be next.

Act 1: Scene III

EXECUTIVE PRESENCE
BY DEFINITION

A s he prepared to begin the session, JT noticed the unusually large number of corporate logos adorning all of the participants' clothes, pens, and notebooks. The group on the right side of the table paid homage to the bold badge of Massive Industries; while the left side displayed the waterfall emblem used by Cascade Incorporated. Between the logos and the way they'd seated themselves to face off across the table, JT knew he had his work cut out for him.

"How many of you came here expecting a lot of depth, substance, and expertise on this career-changing topic, *executive presence*?" JT asked, lobbing his favorite opening line into the charged atmosphere. Three participants' hands went up while the rest sat with arms welded across their chests.

"Those of you expecting a lot of depth all need to lower your expectations because I don't have very much. But I do have style," he said with a flourish.

As expected, some allowed themselves a small smile, but most offered only stony silence. "So tell me…what you were thinking when you heard you'd been 'invited' to training?" JT challenged in his slowest southern drawl.

This time, the group remained silent. No one was even willing to make eye contact. Only the seagulls chose to laugh.

Undeterred, JT continued, "Was it something like, 'Yahoo, executive presence…lucky me?'"

"I can't use the words," Al, the gruff plant manager from Cascade, growled. The group chuckled tensely and nodded their heads in agreement. Al was a stocky, fifty-something guy who looked like he could take on any situation the Cascade manufacturing community could throw at him. Despite the joke, his face and tone reflected his annoyance at being held hostage in this trivial program.

"Thanks, Al," JT responded with a laugh while pounding his hand on his heart. "I appreciate that. The rest of you will be getting out early while Al stays late."

Despite the light-hearted moment, the tension was still thick in the room, so JT continued to prod. "What else did you think? All day and travel time away from your *busy, busy* schedules…."

"It's hard to keep up with the operation," carped Ron from Massive.

"I agree," Ann, Ron's colleague, said between clenched teeth.

"The worst part," Ron continued, "is that it doesn't matter who was delegated to do your work, it's still on your head. Your bosses don't care if you're gone and some idiot drops the ball. You still have to babysit everything."

JT knew this was often the case and did his best to reassure all of them by saying, "I understand, and I'll give you as many breaks as I can today so you can check in. Okay, anything else—good or bad—that you thought when you heard training?" He pushed again.

"Well, to put this into context, understand that I'm in the Massive training and leadership development division," Laleh offered. "So my thought was, this must be an extraordinary program for the company to invest this much time and talent for us." Looking around at all of her fellow participants, she added, "I also thought this must have *tremendous* executive sponsorship." All eyes were on Laleh as she hinted about the elephant in the room.

Silence fell again as each of them considered the company's motives for giving this program such heavy support and why they had been chosen to participate. "Great point, Laleh, let's talk about that for a moment," JT suggested. "Why do you think you were the ones chosen to be here today?"

Instantly the pulse of the room amplified. Though each of them knew why, none wanted to admit it out loud.

JT waited.

Suddenly Ann burst out, "We're here to compete for our jobs."

"I can see why you think that, Ann." JT acknowledged. "However, there's actually a much larger goal for this group." This statement caught them all off guard.

"Yes, today your jobs are on the line due to the merger—there's no denying that. At the same time, each of you is a leader in an incredibly competitive industry, and the reality is that your jobs are on the line *every* day."

Seeing their confused expressions, JT expounded. "Tell me, when are you not competing with: ambitious colleagues, emerging talent willing to work for less, and blazing technologies threatening the need for your position's existence?" He paused.

"Ladies and gentlemen, this program is far more than an extended interview; this is an executive presence boot camp. This program is not about who stays or goes from your newly merged organization…it will determine who among you will be able to remain relevant in today's marketplace." JT had definitely gotten their attention.

"I am often asked, 'Why is executive presence important?' And my answer is this: Executive presence is critical because the competition has never been greater. As evidenced by the people in this room, there are a lot of smart, savvy people out there competing for great positions. Therefore, there could not be a more relevant time than right now to focus on your personal brands.

"In speaking with your leadership, I was told, 'We've all spent so much time branding the company, we've forgotten to brand ourselves, and that's why we need you to guide our teams through a personal branding program.' I thought that was a very profound statement." After pausing to let them consider the thought, JT continued. "Every one of you in this room has a great brand, or you wouldn't be at these terrific companies. It's easy to see that. But it's not enough to just maintain the status quo. To stay relevant, you have to constantly strengthen your brand."

Revealing his protective instincts, David said, "I'd just like to say along the lines of that point: After all of the layoffs Cascade has been through, not to mention the recession, we're not getting rid of poor performers anymore. There are no poor performers left. Now, there's nothing left but the worst of the best."

"The same can be said of our Massive staff," Andrei fired back. Though unlike David, Andrei's motivation was fueled not by a need to protect, but rather by his desire to count coup.

"And that's my point," JT interjected as he stepped into the sight line between the two. "This is a critical time, despite all that you have happening and despite the two hundred plus emails waiting for you in your inbox, to really focus in on your career. This is about your personal development.

"So what is executive presence? How do we define it? As you know, each of you was asked to complete a pre-course survey. One of the questions on the survey asked you to define executive presence. I've chosen two of the definitions to review. Here's the first one:

Executive Presence is someone who commands the attention of others through communication, presenting ideas, delivering information, or recommending change. [Those with] Executive Presence demonstrate strong knowledge about their expertise, use verbal and non-verbal skills to convey information, and have a personal style that is reflective of their presence.

"Sounds strong to me, don't you think?" They all nodded their agreement. "I especially appreciate that this person included the phrase, 'recommending change.' After all, our effectiveness as leaders is measured in large part by our ability to influence the actions of others, is it not?" Again, they nodded.

"Here's the next one:

Portraying confidence when presenting and speaking to others in meetings or on conference calls. Remaining in control.

"I chose this one because of the last two words, 'in control.' If I had to give you the ultimate definition of executive presence, this would be it—having control and command of the room."

JT went on to clarify, "Of course I'm talking about control and command with confidence and assertiveness, not arrogance or aggressiveness. To me, executive presence comes down to that. Even if there are those who are senior to you in the audience, if it's your presentation or meeting, it's your job to stay in control and command of the room."

JT paused, wanting them to fully absorb this idea. "Your executive presence is on display every day when you're giving presentations, leading meetings, or speaking one-on-one to your direct reports. The reason we're here is to make sure that you are the best of the best, so you can stand out in this incredibly crowded marketplace.

"I know you're all under extreme pressure; however, I'd like to ask you to temporarily suspend your relationship to Massive and Cascade, as well as to your titles. Instead, spend today focusing on: Brand Andrei, Brand David, Brand Ann, Brand Laleh, etc. This is your opportunity to define your place in the business world. It would be a shame to miss it."

Reading their body language, JT could see that Laleh, Ajay, and Mizuki were thirsty to learn. He could also see that Ann, Ron, and Al had moved from hostile to resigned acceptance of the situation. As for the gladiators, Andrei and David, it was obvious there was trouble on the horizon.

Act 1: Scene IV

THE BLACK SHEEP

Launching into his trademark introduction, JT began, "A little bit about me: I named my company Black Sheep because I am literally the black sheep of my family. My dad is a GM car dealer, so I tried selling Buick LeSabres for the most miserable thirteen months of my life. If you know how to make to make a Buick LeSabre sound cool, please tell me because I simply could not pull it off," he added, feigning sadness.

"I walked in one day and quit. I told my dad that I simply could not push another Buick or Pontiac or GMC. He was going to cut me out of his will, but my mother fought (and won) to keep me in." At this point, JT dropped into his best used-car salesman voice, "So, please be sure to visit your local GM dealerships. On behalf of my family, I thank you."

Behind him, a slide popped up with a photo of the cast from the television show *Dynasty*. JT explained, "When I was very young,

14

I moved to Hollywood and worked on the primetime television soap opera—*Dynasty*. I'm sure a few of you remember that show."

Pointing over to the now smiling Al, JT went on to say, "Al is looking very intently at the photo trying to figure out which one I am in the picture. Al, I was not a member of the cast; I was never pretty enough for television." A friendly snicker was heard throughout the room.

"I was an assistant to Aaron Spelling, which was a terrific opportunity as he was the most successful TV producer in history at that time. I love to tell people that every day for four years I worked with the beautiful actress Heather Locklear."

Turning his attention back to Al, he said, "Tell me, Al, which way do you think my career is going? I used to work with the beautiful Heather Locklear, and now I work with Tom Harris." As he spoke, a slide came up showing side-by-side photos of Heather and Tom (a sixty-something executive).

For the first time, the group burst into laughter. A couple of them even uncrossed their arms and relaxed.

"While in LA, I hosted an entertainment talk show where I interviewed people from daytime television. Then I moved to Birmingham to be a TV anchor and reporter at the CBS and Fox affiliates. This is where I learned *a lot* about executive presence."

Pausing, JT dropped his volume and told them, "Being in television means getting on camera in the midst of a crisis and informing the public about some difficult event or disaster. As I'm sure all of you know, few things will test your ability to exude executive presence like the task of delivering bad news to people." All heads nodded affirmatively.

"My clients include: GE, Lockheed Martin, American Airlines, Procter & Gamble, Nielsen, NBC Universal, and, of course, Mass Corporation. Please note whose logo is up front and center," JT said, highlighting the Massive Industries image on his logo-laden slide. "Of course, next week when I'm at GE, guess whose logo is going to be up

front and center? That's right, GE. It's called customizing a program."
More laughter.

"I've trained several NASCAR drivers how to talk to the media,
primarily working for Hendrick Motorsports." Choosing to ignore the
sneer on Andrei's face, JT continued, "I assure you those are very smart
people who know a lot about how to authentically sell their brands."
David vigorously nodded his agreement.

Speaking to the next slide, JT said, "I've also had clients who have
appeared on major network news programs. And finally, whenever I'm
not here at my retreat center or in one of the twenty countries I work in
across the world, once a month, on live television, I draw the winning
lottery numbers in my home state." Demonstrating his best game show
host voice, JT said, "Tonight's winning lottery numbers are...."

Though still a bit tight, each of them was loosening their proverbial
collars. Standing to the side so they could read the text on the screen, JT
said, "The single greatest testimonial I've ever had from a client is this:

*At the beginning, JT was nothing but pure entertainment, but
near the end of his session, I realized he actually does have a
little substance.*

"That came from an engineer, and believe me, if an engineer says you
have substance, then you have something going for you." JT's comment
was met with more friendly laughter, and he knew the group was now
ready to proceed into the program.

Act 2: Scene I

TAKING CONTROL AND COMMAND

The brain starts working the moment you are born and never stops...until you stand up and speak in public.

—Anonymous

JT gave them a minute to read the quote on the screen. "What happens to people? Why do we have this fear?" JT posed.

"Afraid of saying something wrong," Laleh answered immediately, demonstrating that she had no such issue.

"Yes...what else?"

"Afraid of rejection or having our thoughts put down," Mizuki, the other twenty-something, quietly added.

"That's true, isn't it, Mizuki?" JT agreed. "Of our idea not being bought. Of them thinking less of us as a leader. What else? What else causes people to be so incredibly nervous?"

Ajay, the recent Cascade transfer to the US, finally ventured into the conversation saying, "You can feel self-confident, but then you get in front of a room full of people and suddenly everything changes. And now, everyone can see you're *not* self-confident. So you're not projecting yourself the same way you see yourself."

"That's right, Ajay," JT affirmed, glad to have Ajay participating. "And from my experience, I believe a lot of that happens because you're not as prepared as you need to be." A guilty wave washed over the group. All of them could easily recount a multitude of situations where they had raced in to lead a meeting with zero preparation.

Knowing what they were thinking, JT offered, "Please know, I realize you don't have hours upon hours for extensive preparation, and I am very respectful of that. But there are things we can do very quickly to move the needle significantly. I'm going to give you some quick tips to move you forward. I'd also like to say this: I think you underestimate yourselves. I think there are times when you know more about your topic, that project, or that product than anyone else in that room, including the senior leaders and clients. But because of their position of authority, you begin to doubt yourself and then the fear of not saying the right thing or not saying it the correct way sets in. But when it's your topic, and you're prepared, that's when you're in control and command of the room."

Act 2: Scene II

BUILDING CONFIDENCE

Nobody ever sold anybody anything by boring them to death.
—**David Ogilvy**, founder, world-renowned PR firm

"How many of you have seen a boring presentation at Massive or Cascade?" JT inquired. "How many of you have been responsible for delivering some of those boring presentations?" Chuckles and groans filled the air. "Well, I'm here to tell you, we can no longer afford to be boring. The competition is too stiff. So what does it take to be a good communicator? What do you have to do?"

"Listen," Laleh answered, her eyes subtly directing her response toward Andrei.

"Yes, Laleh, you certainly must listen. You also have to be able to read the audience. And how hard is that when you're on conference calls and you can't see them?" He asked rhetorically.

"Confidence," Andrei offered, countering Laleh's commentary on him.

"Absolutely, Andrei," JT agreed, overlooking the exchange. "Belief in the product," David countered.

"Yes," affirmed JT, "and aren't there times, David, when you have to deliver a message from corporate that you don't necessarily support?"

"Oh God, yes." David confirmed. "Especially this past year."

Al joined in, "There was a recent situation where I was told to give a presentation, and by the time the meeting was all set up with the presentation ready to go, the whole thing changed because of a new directive. So here I was with this presentation, and half of it was null and void already."

"We will address what you do when you walk in with a great presentation, or so you think, and on the spot, it gets sliced up," JT assured Al.

"It has to be fluid," interjected Ron. "You have to know what your subject matter is and be able to adjust it according to your audience."

"That's right, Ron, because what we want to avoid is having it look choppy," JT said. "When it feels choppy, you look nervous."

Al continued, "That was the thing in my scenario. I had no confidence in what I was saying because I knew most of the stuff wasn't going to work the way I was presenting it."

"Let's go back to what Andrei said. Say it one more time for us, sir."

"Confidence."

"Yes, *confidence*. People often ask me, 'How do I get more confidence?' The answer is really quite simple—you have to earn it. I don't know any other way. It comes when you're prepared, when you manage Q&A well, and when you read your audience. If there's a magic pill out there, please let me be the one to discover it. I know I could sell it. But until we find that pill, there's only one way I know to get it. Confidence comes when it's earned."

Act 2: Scene III

MINUTE TO WIN IT

"**S**o who's ready to build their confidence? I need a volunteer." JT was met with silence. "Let me tell you, there is only one way to get good at this, and that's having a live audience. I promise, this won't hurt, and all of you are qualified for the challenge."

More silence.

"Are you really going to leave me alone up here?" JT asked them.

After another moment of silence, Ron reluctantly stood up and joined JT.

"Thank you, Ron."

"Okay, now I need a timer. Al, would you please time Ron using your phone?" Al nodded his agreement.

"Ron, what I'd like you to do is spend the next thirty to sixty seconds telling us about yourself. We're going to time you, but we're not going to tell you how long you took until afterwards."

Turning back to the participants, he added, "I would like to ask that the rest of you try to gauge how long he speaks without using any clocks. When he's done, please write down your guess at his time. The stage is yours, Ron."

"Okay, well, ah, let's see...." Ron thought out loud. "I'm Ron Johnson, and I've been at Massive for twenty years. I'm the Director of Purchasing. Hmmm... ah...well, I guess I can tell you...um...ah, okay, what I can say is that at this point, my wife and I have quit unpacking because every time we try to set up a home, I get transferred."

At a loss for words, Ron shuffled his feet. "I'm sorry, JT, but I'm Scandinavian, and I just don't think I'm ever going to get the hang of talking about myself. My mother would have taken me to task if she'd ever heard me blowing my own horn like this."

"I understand, Ron," JT said as he walked over to join him. "In fact, I'll venture that most of us feel that way, correct?"

"Yeah, sure, you betcha!" Al mocked Ron with a stereotypical Scandinavian response.

Ron responded with a genuine smile and a gesture of disrespect.

JT laughed, happy to see them teasing each other across company lines. "No worries, Ron. Remember Al is going to be up here in just a minute, and payback is fair play. Let me say this as a learning point for all of us. The key to success with this exercise is not to become puffed up with arrogance, but rather to start gaining comfort with letting people know about our successes." Addressing the group he continued, "Everyone please remember it's impossible to stand out if we're not willing to allow even a small spotlight to shine on us. And folks, in this crowded marketplace, only the standouts will survive."

Bringing his attention fully back to Ron, JT asked, "By the way, Ron, how long do you think that took?"

"Hmm...well it felt like an hour, so I'd probably say two minutes," Ron estimated.

"What did the rest of you write down…Ajay?"

"I thought it was thirty-four seconds," Ajay replied.

"I think it was longer," said Andrei. "I guessed fifty-five seconds."

"Al, how long did Ron take?"

"Thirty-two seconds," Al answered to Ron's surprise.

"And that's one of the reasons why we do this exercise, so we can get a feel for how long thirty to sixty seconds is. If you practice using a timer, you'll find your natural rhythm within that time frame."

"Thank you, Ron," JT said. "It takes courage to be first, and we all appreciate your willingness to let us learn alongside of you."

As Ron returned to his chair, JT added, "Sometimes, as speakers, we can think things are taking far longer than they actually are. When that happens, we'll tend to start rushing," JT could see their heads nod in agreement. "If any of you find yourself in a hurry, take a deep breath, relax, and then speak. That breath will never be as long to the audience as it is to you. Now I need one more volunteer."

More silence. A wave crashed out on the beach, then another.

"Mizuki?" JT prompted, wanting to bring her further into the group dynamic and a step away from her copious note-taking. Mizuki looked up with surprise and then made her way to the front.

"Al, if you would once again keep time. Mizuki, whenever you're ready."

"I'm Mizuki. I am in my first year at Cascade, and I am new to the US," she paused and dropped her head to her chest.

Initially, JT thought she might be experiencing a severe case of stage fright. However, she looked so calm, he decided to give her a chance to move through it.

With her next breath, she raised her head and spoke.

"Please forgive me for keeping you waiting. As I stand here, I am realizing I have never had anyone ask me to speak only of myself." Her eyes danced around the room as though searching for land in these unchartered waters. "The whole idea of it feels quite foreign."

Seeing confusion on some of the faces in her audience, Mizuki explained. "In my homeland, we are taught to remain within the whole. We are not accustomed to 'standing out' this way."

Taking another moment to consider JT's request, she said, "I believe I would like to attempt this exercise again, perhaps after I've had a chance to practice. May I have another opportunity later?"

"Absolutely," JT affirmed.

As Mizuki turned and walked back toward her seat, Ann was struck by how brave the young woman was to have even attempted the exercise, especially considering her heritage. Ann was pretty sure she wouldn't have been able to do it when she was Mizuki's age. In fact, the only way she'd learned to get through her own fears was to charge up front and start barking out orders. "Thank you, Mizuki," she said softly. "Thank you for reminding me that courage doesn't have to be loud or aggressive."

Andrei scoffed at Ann and her typical American sentimentality.

JT returned to his post saying, "I encourage all of you in this room to really think about this. While we may not share Ron's or Mizuki's cultural history, we do all share in the struggle to authentically present our brands and ourselves to others. And just as Mizuki pointed out, it takes practice and preparation to become skilled at it."

"Now let me ask you this, Ron and Mizuki, what about the element of the time? How did it feel knowing you had a time limit?"

"Stressful," Ron quickly answered.

"I did not think about it initially. But then I became quite conscious that I'd gotten lost in time," Mizuki responded.

"I hear both of those answers frequently during other classes, and they bring up another point of this exercise. Having a clock running will help make you a better speaker. It forces you to edit your words and pay attention to your message."

Dropping his voice to the most serious tone he'd used thus far, JT added, "There's a third point to that little role play we asked them to do." Pens stopped as all eyes turned to look at him. "Did you notice that it took me a while to get two volunteers?" They nodded their heads, acknowledging his point.

"If you're serious about building your executive presence, you should fight to get in front of every audience you possibly can. Please don't ever miss an opportunity to get up and authentically promote yourself and your brand. It's simply too expensive not to do so, and no one can afford not to jump at the chance."

"Is that what you mean by the term, 'Unleash Your Best Self?'" asked Ajay.

"Yes, Ajay. Unleashing your best self—or as we like to call it: unleashing your black sheep—is a formula for establishing and expressing your authentic brand of leadership. It's demonstrating executive presence in every communication. From taking control and command, to influencing and inspiring others into action. It's being memorable in a way that makes you stand out from the sameness of the crowd." JT smiled. "And, of course, it's about maintaining your sense of humor at all times."

"Now, let's talk about another useful way to have high impact in only sixty seconds," JT offered. "When you first meet someone, what do you say or do to be memorable?"

"Are you talking about an elevator speech?" Ron questioned back.

"It sounds like it, doesn't it, Ron?" JT said with a smile. "However, what I'm referring to is less about giving a practiced speech and more about *connecting* with someone within the first sixty seconds—what I like to call your Minute to Win It." Ron's quizzical expression remained.

"What if you ended up on the elevator with your CEO? What would you talk to him or her about? Listen to me very carefully: If you even *think* about talking about the weather, I'm coming back! I can hear my boarding call in the airport now, 'Priority Access, now boarding.' *Please* don't talk about the weather unless there's been a major weather event. What you need is not trite commentary; what you need is a connector. Whether it's in an elevator or a chance meeting in the hallway, be prepared with something that connects you to that person. That way you can authentically say:

> 'Andrei, I watched your presentation last week on our webcast, and I especially liked your point about new markets we will explore this year.'

"That's one version. Maybe it's something your CEO said in a newspaper story you really liked that was related to something your team is working on. Whatever it is, you need to have one connector because when you have one connector, you will have a better elevator speech moment, I guarantee you. Quick story," JT offered in explanation. "Not long ago I was preparing a keynote speech when I was informed that a vice president for one of my biggest clients was speaking at the same conference. I'd never met this person of enormous influence and immediately began planning out what I would say should the opportunity to introduce myself arise.

"In just a few minutes of internet research, I discovered there were several people on her team that I already knew—in fact, one of them was a proponent of mine. I was thrilled because this mutual *connection* gave me an easy way to make a memorable impression.

"As it turned out, I was leaving the auditorium when I saw her standing by the door, chatting with someone. I knew she was finished speaking, so I decided to risk waiting around, and it paid off. She entered the lobby, and I was able to approach her." Extending his hand toward Ann, JT demonstrated:

> "Hello, Pamela. I've had the pleasure of working with Manuel Rodriguez from your Latin America team. My name is JT of Black Sheep Consulting." He paused while shaking Ann's hand. "We just missed meeting a few months ago when we were both on the docket at the Corporate Leadership meeting in New York, but I was able to catch your speech. You had quite a response to the new product launch.

"Okay, tell me what I've just accomplished with that connector?"

"You've let her know you have a mutual acquaintance," Andrei said.

"That's right, Andrei. I don't assume she'll walk away remembering my name, but she may remember the guy who knew Manuel. Though it's a long shot, she could even mention it to Manuel...what else?"

"You told her you presented at the Corporate HR Leadership meeting," David said. "I'm guessing not every vendor does that."

"Absolutely," JT affirmed. "In my research, I was reminded that she spoke, and that helped me remember both what she said and the powerful response she received. So what do you think? Was this an average elevator speech where I listed off my qualifications or was this a connection where I planted a seed for a new relationship? Did I leave her with enough of an impression so she may remember me the next time we meet?" Heads nodded.

"In this case, I know she remembered because I saw her again a few months later at another function. I was standing in a hallway, waiting to deliver a keynote." Acting out his story, JT tapped his fingers together, checked his watch, and pretended to wave to an acquaintance. "Hearing footsteps behind me, I turned around to discover it was her, the same

VP, and she was headed directly towards me. Instinctively, I stuck out my hand and said:

'Good morning, Pamela. We met last month in New York. I'm JT of Black Sheep Consulting.'"

As he acted out the memory, JT's body was stiff, and his words were accompanied by a friendly, though slightly strained, smile.

"Today I'm here doing a session on executive presence before you speak at eleven."

Transforming into his nemesis, JT altered his voice and posture into one that exuded power. "Yes, I know. I read the agenda, and I'm coming to sit in on your session."

JT's legs wilted beneath him in feigned horror as he returned to playing himself. "Do you know what I'm thinking on the inside? *The next hour is going to make or break my career.*" Pause. "A single email from this top executive, and I'd stop getting contracts from every division. On the inside, I was incredibly nervous. Losing this client would be catastrophic for my business."

As one, the group nodded with understanding and sympathy. They'd all experienced career-altering situations. In fact, one of them had landed in today's program as a result of foiling a moment like this.

"Well," JT went on to say, "she came in and stayed the hour. Afterwards, she left very quickly without a word of feedback, and I thought, *that's it, I'm done. She didn't like it, and that's all it's going to take to remove me from their vendor list.*

"I was devastated, convinced my nerves had betrayed me. I had friends in the room who said you'd never have known I was nervous, but I knew I'd been internally jumpy because this keynote was my defining moment with this company. Seeing no clear opportunity for damage control, I decided to head to the auditorium to hear her speak. Addressing a standing-room-only audience, she opened with something to this effect: 'Good morning. Before I start my presentation, let me just tell all of you now that I am going to mess up a few things based on what I just learned in JT's session.'" Wiping his brow with the handkerchief from his pocket, JT took a deep breath of relief, just as he'd done that day.

"Today, she will answer an email from me...and she'll do so within an hour. That's the power of an effective connector. She meets a lot of people. Your senior leaders and clients meet a lot of people. What do you do to be memorable? Confident? What do you do in that first minute?" Reaching for his coffee cup, he gave them a moment to ponder the question.

"Now it's your turn. I'd like each of you to take a moment to think about specific people or job titles you're going to be meeting as the merger progresses. Please choose one, and then prepare a connector for that introduction. Then each of you is going to get up and introduce yourself to us as though we were that person or held that title." The assignment was met with a chorus of muffled groans.

"You know what I hear from participants? I hear that this and the last exercise are the toughest ones in the entire session. Why do you think that is? What do you have to get up and sell?"

"Yourself," Al answered with a shudder.

"Yes, yourselves. You can talk all day long about Massive or Cascade, but the real task is how do you authentically sell your own brand?"

"This is the painful part," Ajay stated.

"It is painful," JT acknowledged. "But that's all right. You're with friends. You're going to get feedback, as well as a chance to practice, and it's practice that makes everybody better. Who would like to go first and just get it over with?"

"I'll do it," volunteered Laleh, her fearlessness spawning jealousy amongst some of her elders.

"Laleh, please tell us who you're meeting—in other words, who are we as your audience?"

"You are the Massive committee I am interviewing with next week." Her carefree tone caused another surge of envy from those terrified of having to interview for the first time in years.

JT instructed, "Okay, please listen to Laleh, and note what is interesting to you. What makes her memorable?"

"I love connecting dots, I love connecting people, and I really love creating wonderful work environments. My name is Laleh Patel, and I am a Regional Director of Training & Leadership Development at Massive, Inc. One of my fondest professional memories is when I was assigned to a team of random people pulled together to build a new division. It was an incredible situation because we all took risks. We had to because we had no idea what we were doing." She said with a laugh. "Despite being terrifying, the situation brought out everyone's talents." Laleh paused, smiling warmly. "Today, whenever I run into one of those teammates, we always reminisce about that time and what a great experience it was for all of us." After pausing again, she added, "My goal in this new role, should it be offered to me, is to lead my team with the same emphasis on creative problem-solving I enjoyed with that project. Thank you."

A brief, intimidated applause followed Laleh's introduction.

Voicing everyone's thoughts, JT asked, "Don't you just hate when the people from the training department go first and knock it out of the park?"

"Yup," Al responded.

JT marched on. "We're going to give some feedback now. What are your thoughts about Laleh's introduction to the interview committee?"

"I liked her enthusiasm." Al offered in an ironically subdued tone. "She was so enthusiastic in what she said. Very good vocally."

"Great eye contact," David said, noting that she'd managed to connect to him despite his seat being almost too close for comfort.

"What about her content?"

"I liked how she opened with 'connecting the dots,'" Mizuki observed.

"Mizuki, I'm going to jump on that one for a moment, if I may. Tell me, when you meet somebody for the first time and they say, 'Hello, I'm John Doe from blah, blah, blah.' Do you really remember that person's name?"

The group responded with a non-committal collection of *no*s.

"I agree, and I'm convinced it's because in the first three to seven seconds, we are so busy forming a first impression that we don't hear what they say. We're too busy assessing them. What Laleh did beautifully, and I love it when people can do it, is she had an opening statement, and she gave us her name on sentence three. This technique works even if I were meeting Andrei for the first time one-on-one in the hallway:

Andrei, I'm glad I have the opportunity to meet you. John thought it would be important for us to connect because of our upcoming project together. I'm JT. I'm with the HR department here at Massive.

"I think he has a better chance of remembering because I gave him a reason. 'John thought it would be important for us to connect.' I should add that I don't think you can go past sentence three because after a while you're thinking, *who is this person talking and not telling us who he is?* So, getting back to Laleh, what made her memorable?"

"Her confidence," Ann answered.

"How so?" JT inquired.

"I often find people in her age range come off as cocky. Especially when they have the depth of education she has," Ann's eyes revealed her thoughts as she stole a glance at Andrei. "But she doesn't seem the least bit arrogant, and that's one of the things that makes her stand out in a positive way."

"What makes her appear confident, Ann? Is there something you can put your finger on?"

"It's more a feeling than anything, but if I had to name physical traits, I would agree with David and say it's her eye contact. She also used a very conversational tone. I felt more like she was talking to me than at me. I also really appreciated her passion for her work."

"If you were a member of the interview committee would you want to know more?"

"Definitely," Ann affirmed.

"Then mission accomplished, Laleh. Well done."

"All right, so we've seen the ringer in the group. Who amongst the rest of us mere mortals is ready to learn?"

Without hesitation, Al stomped up to the front, closed his eyes, and leapt. "My name is Al. I'm a plant manager for Cascade Corporation. I've been on the job for thirty-two years…." He sighed and looked over at JT. "I know you keep talkin' about this brand business, but I got nothin'. I'm just an ordinary guy from Boston who goes to work every day and will probably retire before all this is over."

"Al, how long did you say you've been with Cascade?" JT asked. "Thirty-two years."

"And how many hours do you average a week?"

"Around sixty—but then, I take vacations, so let's say fifty."

"Can anyone do a quick calculation for me on how many hours that is?"

Ron grabbed his phone and answered, "At fifty hours a week, that's eighty-three thousand, two-hundred."

Stepping up to stand beside Al, JT said, "It's a pleasure to meet with all of you today. My name is Al Taylor, and I've invested eighty-three thousand hours of my life into the Cascade Corporation. One of my favorite memories is…." Stepping over to the side, JT motioned for Al to fill in the blank.

"When I was promoted to plant manager," Al said, with only a slight hesitation. "I'm the third generation of my family to work at Cascade, and no one else in our family ever made it to plant manager." Al smiled and dropped his head bashfully. "Yeah, it was a great day when I walked over to tell the old man I'd gotten the job. He didn't say much, but I knew he was proud."

"Is this guy memorable or what?" JT asked the group. They responded with applause.

Act 3: Scene I

P.O.W. POWERFUL OPENING WORDS

"It's time to put your communications savvy to the test," JT announced with a mischievous grin. "We're going to be taking a quiz, and I have a prize for the winner that comes straight from my state lottery."

"The winning numbers?" Ron inquired cynically.

"All I can tell you, Ron, is that it's from the lottery," JT answered mysteriously as he handed out a quiz for them to take. "I will also say that some of these questions have more than one right answer, and some of them have only one answer that I will fight to the bitter end to defend.[2]

"All right, so here we go! Keep track of your answers and let's see who wins the big prize:

<hr>

2   Scan this QR code to take the quiz.

Question 1
You should start presentations or meetings by sharing your
program topic in the first sentence. For example, it's okay to start
by saying 'Today, I'm going to give you a status update on....'
a. True
b. False

No one spoke, spurring JT to assume an exasperated posture and say, "When I hear, 'Today, I'm going to walk you through,' I want to walk right out the door because I know I'm about to be 'averaged' to death. Please hear me when I tell you, you have to grab your audience with your *very first sentence*. You have to verbally yank their minds away from the one hundred emails they have lying unopened in their inbox or the conference call they have at two o'clock for which they're not prepared. In today's 'I want it now world,' you have to be engaging in sentence one."

A red circle appeared on the screen highlighting the answer: B. False.

"Ajay, you mentioned that when you're speaking, it's often difficult to be the self-confident person you believe you are?"

"Yes," Ajay tentatively answered, praying JT wasn't about to call him up to the front of the room.

"When do you find yourself the most nervous?" JT inquired.

"Right at the beginning...my palms sweat, my brain goes blank, and my mouth gets really dry." Ajay answered, reaching for his water.

"Thank you for being so forthcoming, and let me say, that's exactly what I hear from clients all the time. I propose that having an average open is what's causing some of your nervousness. If you have a strong, well-thought-out open, you'll be a superstar whether it's on a stage or on a call. Let me give you some examples I know have worked effectively for many of my clients, including Massive executives."

On a slide behind him, a bulleted point appeared:

- Use an email

"Consider doing this to open up your next staff meeting." JT grabbed a piece of paper and began "reading" it:

"Good morning, everyone. I'd like to share an email I got from the CEO this morning at 7:53am. It's written to me, but I really think it's meant for all of us.

"How much more effective is it to have the proof right there? Show them the email because then you bring the CEO right into the room. I find this far more engaging than just telling them about it."

A second slide appeared:

- Tell them something new

"If there is some piece of news that has happened between last Monday's meeting and today's staff meeting and not many people in the room know about it, there's your POW. Please let me be clear, good POWs don't have to be dramatic or grand. They just have to be a little different. They have to be *interesting*. This idea came from one of my CEO clients who said, 'JT, I go to these weekly staff meetings with my team, and I walk out of there thinking, *that was a re-hash of what we did last week and the week before*.' Do you ever feel the same way?" Heads nodded.

"Of course, you do," JT stated, filling in his own blank. "That's why it's critical to tell an audience something they don't know right up front in order to pull them in."

A third bullet appeared:

- Recalibrate the audience

"This technique is outstanding whenever time has passed. In this scenario, Mizuki is my boss," JT said, pointing over to the blushing Mizuki.

JT smiled and continued, "She asked me to work on this project four weeks ago. I've not seen much of Mizuki as she's been traveling a lot. I'm now back in her office on a Monday morning presenting on the project she asked me to explore. In this case, my POW to her would be:

Mizuki, four weeks ago you asked my marketing team to look at new strategies around our online presence. I have three strategies I want to present to you today and quite frankly, Mizuki, I think you're going to be surprised by one of them.

"Why would it work, when four weeks has passed, for me to use that as my set up to that meeting?"

"It's something new," Al said.

"You've piqued her interest," David stated.

"Intrigue," Ann responded.

"Yes, you're all right," JT agreed. "Being a good communicator is a little bit of intrigue, drama, and suspense. You have to make them want to hear what's coming next, which is why I said, 'I think you're going to be surprised by one of them.'

"But what was the other purpose of me doing that? Bear in mind, four weeks have passed." JT held up four fingers to reiterate his point.

"It reminds her of the assignment she gave you," Al offered again.

"And helping her remember is a good place to start, isn't it, Al? All day long she asks people to do things. Would it be wise for me to assume she remembers our meeting from a month ago, when we've had little interaction and no discussion on this topic? I wouldn't want to take that risk. I'd much rather recalibrate, so I can be assured we're on the same page. I'd do this with the senior executive team just as I would one-on-

one with Mizuki, my boss, in her office. This POW also works well with large groups when it's been a while since we've gathered and I was tasked to come back with information.

"There's another advantage to this approach. How many of you feel like you're presenting to senior leaders and you're hardly through forty seconds when someone interrupts you with a question?" Every hand went up.

"Based on what you just saw me do with Mizuki, doesn't it seem like it would be harder for her to interrupt me? After all, I'm providing her with exactly the information she asked me to give her. Wouldn't it make sense for her to listen? When you set up your presentation with a recalibrating POW, you have reduced the likelihood of her interrupting you in the first thirty to sixty seconds. Sure, the hand is going to go up, but this method may buy you more listening time. By the way, do you ever have leaders at Massive who say to you, 'Got it?'"

"Never," Ron responded sarcastically. "Yes, they say, 'Got it' or 'I get it.' I hate that."

"I understand it's annoying, but when they say, 'Got it' or 'I get it,' please do not say another word about anything on that slide. When you hear 'got it,' that means click and move to the next slide. All too often, I see people who get so attached to their material that they forget to adjust to the situation. Please don't do that to your brand. You never want to be marked as a presenter who doesn't know when to move on. Now, let's move on." JT said with a smile.

- Let someone or something else make your point

"This POW strategy came from another client of mine. His company had gotten some results from a customer satisfaction survey, and he wanted his senior leadership team to fully appreciate the nature of the feedback. Here's what we did.

"He chose eight comments that were very disparaging to the company. We then gave each comment its own slide and put them into slideshow mode. As the meeting attendees entered the room, the stream of negative comments greeted them in a forty-eight-point font on a fifteen square foot screen. My client told me the execs walked in chatting and laughing until the images stopped them in their tracks.

"Prior to using POWs, my client found he was always a little nervous in the beginning. By placing the POW before he'd said a word, he felt it took the pressure off. It was a beautiful way to set up the meeting and also to deal with some of his nervousness issues."

Getting eye contact with each of them he stated, "Your presentation doesn't start when you stand up here, it starts when the first person walks into the room."

- Tell a story

"When presenting for another client, I asked four separate groups to identify one of their own whom they considered to be a great speaker. Despite the fact that the trainings took place in different cities—Orlando, Atlanta, Los Angeles, and New York—in all four, the same name came up. No, it wasn't the CEO. In fact, this person was a middle manager who didn't have frequent national exposure, making it all the more unusual for him to have gained such a far-reaching reputation. When asked what it was about this speaker that made him so great, every group answered that he always starts out with a quick, relevant story that ties in perfectly with the message he's going to give, and he always appears totally prepared.

"We'll be spending more time on this a little later. But for now, I cannot emphasize enough the power of a good story. You'll want to keep it brief and always be sure to tie it back to your message, so there's no confusion about your point."

JT stepped to the side, so they could see the next bullet point:

• Present an interesting fact or statistic

Dropping into role-play mode, JT said,

"Today, in another division, our firm just launched a product made from an alloy never before used in this product line. That's exactly the kind of innovative thinking I'd like to see regarding our project."

"How would we know something like that?" Ron demanded.

"A company newsletter or the internet," JT answered. "I promise you, if you're willing to spend even just five minutes looking around the 'net, you'll find an interesting piece of information you can use that will make you *memorable*. And that's the whole point—to be memorable, in a positive way, of course." JT paused. Ron was quiet, though he was obviously not convinced.

• Make your case up front

"Have you ever been in a scenario where you're going in to ask for resources, and before you say a word, you know your boss is already planning to say 'no'? Has anyone had that experience?" JT raised his hand as an invitation for them to raise theirs.

Most of them raised their hands. David merely dropped his head and began rubbing his forehead. Ever since this merger nightmare began, he'd had an impossible time protecting his team and budget. Over and over he'd been to meetings begging to retain valuable assets of all forms—to no avail. He doubted anything JT was going to say would help.

"Ajay, I'm going to pretend you're my boss. I'm in the marketing/branding department at Massive, and I'm coming in to ask you for fifty thousand dollars to fund a marketing strategy. It's a terrible time to be asking because the numbers are already down. As I'm preparing for this meeting, I am aware that Ajay has an idea of what I want, and in his mind, his answer is already a firm 'no.' This would be my open in that scenario:

> Good morning, Ajay. Let me get right to the point of why I'm here today. I am asking for fifty thousand dollars to fund a new online strategy we're trying to implement here at Massive. I know some people would say it's a terrible time to be asking because of where we are with the numbers. However, based on the research and analysis I'm going to share with you, I believe there's never been a better time to be asking for this investment. I'm confident I can take this fifty thousand dollar online investment now, and turn it into a three hundred thousand dollar profit for Massive in three months, maybe even less. So in the time you've given me today, Ajay, I'm going to make my case that this is the absolute right time for this investment.

"Why might that have opened him up? What did I say that might have loosened him?"

"Return on investment," Ann stated in a crisp tone.

"Absolutely, Ann." JT agreed. "I put the value proposition right up front. So often I see presentations and meetings where people build this elaborate case before giving the value proposition. When really that just gives Ajay twenty more minutes to be thinking, *no.*

"Whenever you're walking into a pre-determined 'no,' you need to put the most important reason for them to say 'yes' in the first words. That's the only hope that you have of even getting a chance to convince them. What else did I do in those Powerful Opening Words?"

"You caught his attention with a figure," Al offered.

"Yes, Al, I caught his attention. If this is a conference call and he's sitting at his desk looking at an inbox full of emails or thinking about a meeting he has later with the senior leadership, I have to pull him in. I have to stop everything else that's going on in order to convince him that the fifty thousand dollars is a good investment. I also think it beautifully sets him up to keep an open mind or at least to give me a chance to prove that it's the right time."

"Sure, that's all it takes, a few powerful opening words," David mumbled under his breath.

"That's not *all* it takes, is it, David?" JT acknowledged. "A great POW doesn't do the convincing. It simply sets the stage for communication. A POW without executive presence will ring hollow. To be effective, it must be both powerful and authentic. In a few minutes, you'll each be writing a POW, and I whole-heartedly recommend you use one that you fully support. Otherwise, it won't ring true, and your brand won't benefit from it."

David just shook his head.

"David, would you mind giving us an example of a situation you've had to face, so we can develop a POW as a group?" JT lightly challenged.

"Sure," David agreed, doubting JT had the chops to help. "Why not? Here's the situation: I'm in the middle of an immense design project—one I've been working on for the past two years. At this point, I need more funding to complete the project. I also need experts to interpret the research. As you may have heard, we've just merged with a larger company, and so far," he said glaring over at Andrei, "there hasn't been any response from the Massive *machine*."

"All right, so we have our meeting topic." JT intervened, again stepping into the sight line between David and Andrei. "How could we make a case up front that would, at the very least, get David's message heard?"

No one responded.

"This is live ammunition; let's all do whatever we can to lend a hand," JT encouraged them.

"Is your design similar to a competitor's?" Ron asked with a tone intended to sting.

"Yes, though it will be spectacularly more efficient," David shot back.

"David," Ann probed in a neutral manner, "what is the advantage of your project? What would matter to the audience that controls the resources you need?"

David did his best to calm down and explain. "This product is a modified version of what we sell now. What makes it relevant is that our current product is becoming obsolete, and this is very likely going to be the next generation."

Sensing how hot this button was going to be within the group, JT decided to take this on himself. "How about something like this:

> I realize not everyone feels the timing of this project is appropriate due to the merger. However, with the extensive media coverage the merger is getting, there's a strong argument for announcing this project today. Thus, assuring our critics that the new company isn't just going to work out, it's already defining the cutting edge. Will it cost money, yes, but with this much free publicity, can we afford to ignore this opportunity?"

"That certainly puts a different spin on it," Ron said with surprise.

"You know, David, I'm in on a lot of the press activities. I could help you fine-tune an opening like that," Laleh offered.

"That would be great. Thanks!" David responded, feeling his first twinge of hope in months. "It's just occurred to me that for the past year all I've done is play defense to protect my resources. I can see it's time to implement some offense by looking for a context they'll be willing to support."

"And there's another great reason to craft a POW. It helps you connect your message to your audience's needs," JT stated. "Okay, now it's everyone's turn to write a POW for a situation you're currently facing. You only have five minutes for this exercise because that's all you'll have out in the real world."

"Who wants to share their POW with us?" JT invited.

"I will," Andrei volunteered, plugging his computer into the screen. "Andrei, if you would please, tell us who we are as your audience."

"You are our customers, and the point of this meeting is to demonstrate how globalization has affected our company over the past fifty years."

"Whenever you're ready," JT said, stepping off to the side of the room.

On the screen a grainy, black-and-white photo of a dreary place on a dreary day appeared. Pointing to it, Andrei said, "This is my homeland fifty years ago. This is the landscape I grew up in—bleak…barren… void of hope. If I had been caught talking to any of you, I would have been shot."

Next, a colorful photo filled with people at a street fair in the middle of a bustling town flashed up. "This is my homeland today— vibrant, thriving, opportunities abound. And, as you can see, people from all over the globe are now a common sight. What a difference fifty years makes."

You could have heard a pin drop.[3]

---

3   Scan this QR code to receive a list of other Powerful Opening Words.

Act 4: Scene I

MODEL COMMUNICATIONS

"**A**ll right, now that we've had a POW-erfully good time…."
Everyone groaned. "Let's move on." A new slide popped up.

Question 2

*Based on a three-part, scientific communications model
equaling 100%, which of the following is accurate in
determining your impact with an audience?*

    a. What you say   7% out of 100%

    b. How you say it   38% out of 100%

    c. What people see   55% out of 100%

"A, B, or C? Which of these is accurate?" JT posed. A chorus of
answers rang out covering all three of the options. Allowing for a
moment of anticipation, JT highlighted C. "For those of you who
said 'B,' I'll give you this one because it's fairly close. The answer

to this is 'C.' Fifty-five percent of people said what they see has the most impact."

A chart appeared on the screen.

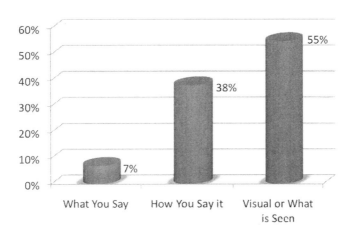

YOUR IMPACT ON AN AUDIENCE

"Let me share this study done in 1967, by Dr. Albert Mehrabian, a Professor of Psychology at UCLA. There's a lot of debate on the accuracy of these types of studies; however, my fifteen years of experience supports their findings. In this study, seven percent is what you say—the actual message, and thirty-eight percent is how you say it—your volume, your vocal quality, your modulation.

"Finally, fifty-five percent is what people see. Visual impact includes: body language, slides, and use of a flip chart or white board. It also encompasses the tools available through WebEx, GoTo, Live Meetings, and other software programs.

"Tell me," JT challenged, "if you had a major presentation next week, which of these three would you probably spend the most time preparing?"

"The content," Andrei answered.

"I understand, Andrei. A lot of people will spend it here," JT stated, pointing to the 'What You Say' bar. "And a lot will spend it here." He pointed to the 'How You Say It' bar. "But I am here to say, you have to focus on all three."

A mixture of affirmative responses rang through the room.

"To be successful today, we have to have the verbal, the vocal, *and* the visual."

Act 4: Scene II

WHAT THEY HEAR

I n a monotone voice no louder than a murmur, JT said, "If I'd started my presentation at eight o'clock this morning using this tone, and I'd spent the whole day talking to you at this volume the entire time, what would many of you be thinking about right now?"

"This is *misery*," Ron answered.

Returning to his usual projection, JT said, "As confirmed by Ron, vocal quality and volume are very important to executive presence. It's better to speak ten percent too loud than one percent too soft. Now let's talk ahs, ums, and filler words. How can you reduce *ah*s and *um*s and fillers that we often use?"

"Pause," suggested Ann.

"Pause, sure, Ann. And may I say, I think it's easier to pause when we create our slides in a way that provides us with natural pauses. What else can you do to reduce your ahs and ums?"

"Be conscious of it," Al answered.

"Being conscious of it, Al. Because oftentimes we don't even know we're doing it. Do we? I will give you a real life example of what happened to me in Atlanta, Georgia, when I was doing this same program. One day, for some unknown reason, I started using a filler phrase that is grammatically incorrect. Instead of ahs or ums, I started saying 'you might should,' or 'you might could.'

"Now, before you judge me, let me tell you, I am aware this is grammatically incorrect. But I am from the South, where we bless everyone's heart, even if we talk badly about him or her. So what can I say? I don't always follow the rules." JT's explanation was delivered in his finest southern twang, making them laugh even more.

"You know what the participants started doing? They kept a flip chart and passed markers around the room. Then any time I said 'might could,' they knocked each other down so they could get over to the board and give me another demerit. And I tell you what, Ajay, I can still hear their, 'Ah, got 'cha,' in my sleep. It didn't take long to cure me because for the first time, I became aware I was doing it.

"If you have a tendency to use filler words, you may need an accountability partner. For example, if I'm concerned about filler words, I should ask Al to cue me. I could say, 'Al, if I say ahs and ums in my presentation, and it becomes distracting, I want you to close your laptop. That's going to be my visual cue that I'm doing this.'

"If you don't get a visual cue within the presentation, you will likely have no idea you're doing it. What else could you do?"

"Prepare and rehearse," Mizuki suggested.

"Yes, Mizuki. Just as we talked about in the introductions," JT agreed. "When you've studied your material and then rehearsed it, you'll use a lot fewer fillers. We fill when we don't know where we're going. Everyone has something to work on; if filler words are your challenge, then that's what you need to do.

"Now for modulation. How do you get good modulation, so you don't sound like this?" JT's voice went flat as his hand drew a straight horizontal line in the air.

"Breathing," Laleh said.

"Pacing," Ann offered.

"Both of those and gestures, as well," JT added, placing his hands in front of his body—ready for action. "The simple act of getting your hands in the right spot will cause your modulation to improve."

"Be enthusiastic," Laleh said.

"Yes! Be enthusiastic. Let your passion come through. And finally, for people whose voices are very even and monotone, one of the best solutions is to share a quick story. When you can bring a story into your meeting or presentation, you will automatically improve modulation. Because stories have characters and drama, and they naturally cause you to change your voice. Think about when you read a bedtime story to a small child."

Demonstrating through a string of altered voices, JT said, "*I'm going to huff and puff and blow your house down!* Or, *then the scary monster poked his head out from the covers and said, 'Boo!'*

"I had one client who practiced reading her speech as though it were a bedtime story. Just running through it that way gave her a sense of where she could add emphasis and vary her modulation. I had another client learn to add natural pauses into his speaking style by reading a newspaper out loud. When you're looking at a newspaper column, how many words are in that column—five or six, right? By having so few words on a line, you automatically slow down because you read the six words, and then you drop down. Versus when it's sixteen words that read straight across a whole page, which allows you to fly through the material."

"JT, I have a question," Ann said rather forcefully. "I acknowledge that the way we speak and the visual we present are relevant, but are you actually saying they're *equal* in importance to *content*?" She'd spent her life disseminating technical information to the less informed. In her world, JT's statements were practically sacrilegious.

"Actually, Ann," JT responded as he walked over to her side of the room. "What I'm saying is that people are heavily persuaded by what they see and hear. Therefore, if we want to make a pitch for someone's time or resources, we need to be very aware of our delivery, body language, and eye contact."

Ann seemed less likely to throw something at JT. At the same time, her posture reflected that she remained devoted to her content.

"May I ask you a question, Ann?" JT inquired.

"Sure," she relented, despite her crossed arms and a slight shrug of her tightly held shoulders.

"What type of requests do you have to make?"

Reluctantly, Ann told him. "My department is currently managing the entire data integration for the merger. What no one seems to get is that this is an enormous process requiring hours and hours of highly skilled labor." Sitting forward, she shook her head with exasperation. "My team was already taxed by the sheer volume of responsibilities we held. Then one day, this...this...*executive*," her words dripped with aggravation, "barges into my office to inform me that I am now in charge of making the merger technologically smooth without saying a word about increasing my workforce or budget."

Having worked herself up, she couldn't help but add, "As if that isn't bad enough, now they've imprisoned me in *communications training*."

Once he was sure she'd finished venting, JT said to her sincerely, "I feel your pain. Unfortunately, I am not in a position to change your situation. What I can offer you is an opportunity to receive feedback for your pitch. That way, at least you'll have gotten the maximum value out of your time here."

Though frustrated, Ann was a reasonable woman, and therefore, she conceded the point.

Seeing her sigh in surrender, JT pounced on the moment. "Ann, would you be willing to share your POW? I think this might be a helpful learning exercise for everyone."

"Certainly," she answered, standing up and moving briskly toward the front of the room. JT was pleased by her enthusiasm as he'd had a hunch she would jump at a chance to temporarily lead.

"My name is Ann, and I'm here to...." Ann stopped speaking when she realized she'd forgotten to use her POW. Quickly she walked back to her place and picked up the paper on which she'd written it down.

She began again, "Massive Industries has approximately four hundred fifty thousand part numbers, eighty thousand employees, ten thousand customers, and four thousand two hundred fifty active software programs. Managing the IT needs of a corporation this size is a full-time job for my team of twenty-five dedicated professionals. As of two days ago, I was informed I have six months to integrate Cascade's electronic data into the Massive structure—an entity approximately twenty-five percent of the size of Massive. Not included in my directive is how this project is going to be staffed and funded. I am here today to inform you of what we need to accomplish this goal, so you can make those determinations. Please wait for one moment while I set up my computer, so we can review each item."

Clapping enthusiastically, JT stepped up next to her, effectively blocking her from actually retrieving her computer. "That was a unique POW, wouldn't you agree?" He asked the audience as they offered a smattering of applause.

Turning to Ann, JT said, "Some of our clients love to use one 'big number' as a way to start off their presentation. Sometimes they will ask it in the form of a question, such as:

'What does the number sixteen million represent?' Answer: 'The number of dollars we left on the table last year for not properly completing our government compliance forms.'

"I've seen some presenters put the number on a PowerPoint slide and nothing else, while they asked the question or told what it represented. The late Steve Jobs of Apple was masterful at using one big number or theme on a PPT slide. One year at a shareholder's meeting, one of his slides featured a large percentage, seventy percent, on the front of a car's windshield. It represented the percentage of US cars that would soon have iPod connectivity. If only other companies could follow this simple, yet compelling, strategy. Now, let's get back to our discussion about the importance of what the audience hears and sees." Motioning toward Ann, he asked, "What did you notice during Ann's presentation?"

"She certainly had very *direct* eye contact," Laleh ventured— her appalled tone leaving little doubt about her uneasiness with Ann's delivery.

"And how important is eye contact?" JT asked, choosing to spin Laleh's observation into a positive lesson for all of them. "It's critical, isn't it? It's one of the most powerful techniques we can use to engage, and thereby influence, our audiences.

"Whenever you present, you want to be sure you connect to as many audience members as possible through friendly eye contact without being forceful about it or staring anyone down."

Having made his point, he took them back on track by asking, "What did you hear when Ann presented?"

"I also felt she really knew what she was saying," Laleh added with a sincere nod to Ann.

"Could you break that down into more detail, Laleh?"

"Hmmm, well, I found the statistics interesting. But you know, I think I was equally influenced by her authoritative tone of voice."

"I completely agree with you, Laleh. Ann definitely has a gift for sounding like the voice of authority—another critical asset to establishing your executive presence," JT concurred. "Other feedback?"

"No offense, Ann, but you seemed a little stiff to me," David observed.

All the Massive employees froze. Ann had a well-deserved reputation as a take-no-prisoners manager who didn't tolerate being challenged. As one their own, the contingent had the urge to protect her. However, they'd each been on the receiving end of her frosty side and were curious to see how someone from Cascade would fare.

Sensing the tension mount in the room, JT knew this hybrid team needed practice exchanging constructive criticism. "What *specific* details about her presentation makes you think that?"

David squirmed in his chair before sharing. "When she stands so straight and doesn't move her hands, well…she just looks stiff or really tense." Ann locked her jaw and acknowledged his critique with a curt nod.

"And how do you interpret that?" JT asked, continuing to dig. "What are you thinking?"

"I'm thinking she may be really nervous, and I'm not sure why. I can't tell if she's uncomfortable speaking or if she's not sure of her information. Sorry, Ann." The mere thought that she could be seen as insecure with her facts caused Ann's entire body to tighten further.

JT wasn't surprised to see Ann recoil, knowing David's comments were a direct hit to her professional Achilles' heel. He also knew if she didn't take charge of this issue very soon, she'd be merger collateral.

"Thank you, David. I know it can be difficult to share authentic feedback with our colleagues—especially with those we *highly respect*." Ann's right eyebrow twitched in acknowledgement of JT's compliment.

"You've brought up a great learning point. When we stand firmly, without any motion of our hands or feet, we can appear stressed. Versus when our bodies are relaxed and fluid, we look more at ease. The more at ease we are, the more engaged we become with our audience and the greater our chances become at having them grant our requests.

"In just a moment, we'll review body language and how we can enhance our stage presence. But first, I want to thank you, Ann. It takes profound courage to open oneself up to the perspectives of others. Overall, I thought you did an outstanding job of getting our attention with relevant statistics. I also thought you established your expertise using an authoritative tone. Finally, I truly appreciate your passion for excellence." Ann thawed enough to give JT a small, but sincere, smile before returning to her chair.

Act 4: Scene III

WHAT THEY SEE

"What would you guess people struggle with the most when they're standing before an audience?" JT asked, waving his hands and fingers.

"Hands," the group answered unanimously, glad to move past the uncomfortable moment between David and Ann.

"Unless you're Italian," Al joked.

"Then we may choose to edit their hand gestures, right, Al?" JT added, gesticulating wildly. "While I don't want anybody to look robotic, I am going to show you what looks good and what does not."

Placing his hands behind his back, pursing his lips, and rocking on his heels, JT asked, "What does this say to the audience?"

"You don't care," David interpreted.

"Yeah, my way or the highway, David—do as you're told. At least that's the potential perception."

Crossing his arms across his chest, JT said, "Of course we all know what people are thinking when we're standing like this before a group. It looks like we're closed to new ideas."

Placing his hands on his hips, he added, "We should avoid this because it looks like we're angry.

"Please don't put hands in pockets. Here you are giving a serious message, and you've got this going on," JT stood with one hand out and one hand in his pocket. "What does this visual say?"

"Nonchalant," David responded.

Giving a nod to David's answer, JT added, "Whatever…no big deal. Please do not do that."

Pausing for a moment and dropping his voice, he continued. "Hear me when I say, I'd never want anyone to think for a moment that I'm trying to create robots. So when I'm talking about making adjustments to your body language, I'm not asking you to adopt a stiff, uniform appearance. What I'm referring to is having your body be congruent to your message. I'd just hate to see any of you inadvertently sabotage your own message by not paying attention to what your audience sees. Remember, perception is everything when we're talking about executive presence.

"Here's what looks good on the stage for anyone." JT stepped into the center of the room to demonstrate. "Your weight is evenly distributed, your shoulders are back, and your hands are right here, resting lightly together just over your belt or lower stomach area. If you're nervous, you can grab one hand with the other. But any time you're not gesturing, this is a good place for them to be. Why? What does this visual say?"

"Confident," Laleh answered.

"Confident, ready, prepared, not afraid to take it on," Andrei agreed.

"And ready to *listen*," Laleh insisted.

"Ready to listen," JT repeated. "There's a very humbling presence conveyed by this position, as well as a commanding presence. And that's what happens, when your hands are right here in front you."

"You're non-confrontational," Al read.

"Yes, you're non-confrontational. I also find that when I can get people to put their hands here, without even realizing it, they will use their hands more effectively. It will bring your message to life and you won't even realize that you're doing it. Your hands will simply work with you.

"Now, do not wash your hands," they all chuckled as he demonstrated his points. "Do not twist wedding bands, do not have a pen in your hand that you click open and closed out of nervousness. *Do not* hold a bottle of water in your hand. You can have a bottle of water, but do not hold it in your hand."

"The only thing really allowed in your hand is the slide remote." He said, holding up his slide remote and then placing it back on a nearby table.

"What I encourage all of you to do is practice in front of a mirror and/or videotape yourself. It will help you get comfortable with the feeling of using your hands to highlight your words." He could see them cringe at the thought of being videotaped. "One of my clients, the CEO of a major corporation headquartered in India, said that seventy percent of all ticks disappear the first time a person sees themselves on video. It's because you don't believe it until you see it.

"How about when you're seated? So much of what you're doing is when you're seated." JT brought a chair over from the side of the room. "Let's talk about this for a moment. Here you are at the conference table, and you have an important point to make. When it's your turn, please sit up. Don't ever make it from the backrest. Because what does this say to the audience?" JT asked leaning back in his chair.

"Whate-v-e-r," David answered, borrowing his teenage daughter's favorite response.

"Exactly, David. It says your point is not worth sitting up and taking notice. When you have something important to say to the audience, come off that back rest."

Sitting up straight, he demonstrated: "You know, Mizuki, I want to comment on your last point because I think it's going to be critical as we set up our budget for fourth quarter.

"This says what to someone?"

"I'm ready," replied Mizuki.

"I'm interested," added David.

"I'm ready; I'm interested; I'm an executive," JT reiterated. "You cannot slouch or lean back when you have an important point to make. It just doesn't match what you're saying and will totally negate it. When I worked in television on the news set they taught us—man or woman—to pull down our jackets and sit on them, if it was long enough. Why do you think they had us sit on our jackets like this?"

"So you couldn't move," Laleh answered.

"Laleh, you're right, it gives you the best posture in the world." As a demonstration, he rocked in his chair as though captured in a straight jacket. "Trust me, I couldn't go back if I wanted to. I'm not going to sit like this for an hour, but when it's my turn to speak, I'm going to make sure that I look the executive with presence.

"By the way, any time you're about to take over the stage, do not leave anyone's work behind you. Even if you're in a situation where it's a group presentation and you're simply taking over, make sure there's not other stuff going on behind you." JT walked over to his flip chart and turned the page.

"One last note on the topic of being careful about what your audience sees," JT added as he returned to the front of the room. "Let's say you put up a slide and notice that your primary stakeholder *does not* like what he or she sees. In fact, for whatever reason this person has become infuriated by the proposal and what they see. Can I tell you what I'd do if that happened to me?"

He walked over to his laptop and hit a key that caused the slide screen to go black. He then said: "Ajay, I'm going to stop right here.

Obviously that was not the right message for today's meeting. Let's just discuss this if we could.

"Get rid of the evidence," JT exclaimed, pounding on the table. "Don't leave something on the screen that is making someone in the audience go crazy." He paused. "I had someone do this in a meeting with his CEO, and he said it saved his career. There was some number on the screen that really hit a nerve, and he knew he needed to abandon his presentation on the spot. Blacking out the visual gave him a chance to change direction instantly.

"So when I went to a black screen just now, what did it do for me?"

"It made the attention come back to you, not the screen," David said.

"Thank you, David. How many of you ever go to a black screen in a presentation?" No one raised a hand.

"*How* did you do that?" Andrei asked.

"I went to a black screen by using the slide remote. However, if I hit the 'B' key on my computer while I'm in PowerPoint slide show mode, it will also take me to a black screen. I can then get it back by hitting the 'B' key again.[4]

"I will tell you if you're doing a face-to-face it can be very effective to start off on the black screen. Think about this—why not get up and do your POW with nothing behind you? And then hit the 'B' key and let it pop back up. That would be different and memorable.

"Though please don't use this tip when on a webinar. People are nervous enough about technology, and they'll assume they've been disconnected or there's been some other problem." Everyone chuckled at the thought.

David offered, "The black screen reminds me of when I went to a concert where halfway through the show, the singer stopped and

4   You must be in slideshow mode, and this is for English. The key varies in other languages depending on the word for black. If you are working in a language other than English, you will need to press F1 to figure out which key to push for the screen to go dark. It is different for each language.

asked everyone to be quiet. He then sang without any instruments or crowd noise. This huge crowd went absolutely silent…and he just sang. It was incredible."

"I love it," JT said. "Do it without all the stuff behind you. If you've never considered the technique of unplugging while making a point then I whole-heartedly suggest you start. After all, who's the messenger here, you or that slide? When you have a compelling point, an interesting fact, or a quick story to share, and it doesn't need a slide, go to a black screen, and feel your control and command of the room grow."

Act 4: Scene IV

VISUAL AIDS

"We've spoken about the visual impact from body language and eye contact, but let's not forget it's also visual aids. So let's talk about the death by PowerPoint. What do you see us doing wrong with PowerPoint at Massive and Cascade?"

"Too many of them."

"Reading the slide."

JT repeated, "Reading the slide, too many of them…."

"Too much on them," Andrei added.

"Too much on them," JT reiterated. "You know, whenever somebody says this to me, 'I know this is really hard to read but…' or 'I know this is a busy slide but…' I always think, *then why is it up there if I can't read it? What was the point?*

"What else? What else do we do wrong?"

"Instead of looking towards the group, we look at the slide and talk about what's on it," David said.

"I have seen people do this. Pretend my cover slide is up on the screen with my name on it." To emphasize his point, JT repeated, "I've actually seen people do this, 'Good morning, everyone. I want to thank you so much for coming today.'" Then turning to the screen, he pretended he was reading, "I'm presenting on Executive Presence. My name is JT." His volume dropped, and he continued to keep his back turned to his audience.

He turned around to face the group and said, "Really, you can't even give me your name and the title of your presentation without having to go to your slide? That's a crutch, and that's what happens to us when we over-use PowerPoint. The problem, as I see it in the clients I coach and presentations I watch, is that people have let PowerPoint become the messenger.

"The other issue is that we're trying to accomplish too many things at once. People want the slide presentation they deliver on the screen to also be a handout, a white paper, as well as a legal document to go in the folder," JT stopped and shook his head. "Use the notes section if you need it for the handout, put it in the appendix, and go to it if you must.

"I have to tell you, a slide presentation deck simply will not be effective for all of those functions. Sometimes you might, as much as you don't want to, do a 'save as' and create a delivery presentation where it's just bullets and photographs. In fact, why should there be a complete sentence on a PowerPoint slide? Unless it's a vision statement or a quote, I ask you to think about why there'd be a complete sentence on a slide.

"Tell me this, if you knew you had a major presentation on Tuesday, and you did something similar to it a month ago, what would all of us be guilty of wanting to do, myself included?"

"Use the one we'd used the month before," David answered.

Nodding his head in agreement, JT said, "We certainly would. We would take the one from a month ago and update it. Today, in this moment, I am begging you to stop that practice. It's the type of habit that can ruin your executive presence.

"There is a much more effective way to put together a presentation. Several years ago a client told me about a great way he set up his presentations. He told me that before he powered up his laptop, he always sat down for five minutes and thought about his message and his audience. He'd think about: *Who will be attending my presentation? Where will the audience be in the decision-making process? What information will they need to take the next step? What will likely be the opposition to my plan or proposal?*

"He claimed that seeing his answers to these questions all on one piece of paper saved him a substantial amount of time. Frankly, I believe if you took five minutes, I think you could save yourself thirty minutes to an hour. Now, your answers to these questions become your storyboard, and that's how you build your slides, with that big visual overview. So when you have too much on your slide, what do you invite from your audience?"

"Too many questions," Ron answered.

"Too many questions and the potential for controversy. The more you put on there, the riskier it gets.

"I am also sympathetic and empathetic to the fact that you all are told this:

'Mizuki, you're going to present Friday at the leadership meeting. I want one slide, and I want these twenty data points covered, got it?'

"What's Mizuki going to do?" JT posed rhetorically. "She's going to put twenty data points because that's what the boss said. However, even if the formatting you have to deliver is out of your control, *how you deliver it* is *in* your control.

"Let's say I'm Mizuki's boss, and I've just asked for one slide with twenty data points. What does Mizuki need to ask me before she leaves my office?"

"Really? You *really* want me to bore them to death with twenty points?" Al asked, getting a laugh out of the group.

"How much time does she have?" Ann demanded to know.

"That's it, Ann. Perhaps the most important question of all, 'how much time do I have?' See I think you're told one slide because they want you to be what?"

"Brief." They answered as one.

"Fine, I'll be brief, but I want to know how many minutes I have. That's a key piece of information. What else should she be asking?"

"How would you like those data points presented?" Laleh asked.

Pointing to Laleh, JT agreed, "Is there an order of priority? What do you think is the most compelling message? Could you tell me a little bit more about the audience? Who might ask tough questions, etc., etc.? It's all in the preparation."

"So now I'm going to play Mizuki." Pointing to her, JT said, "You're going to play me, your boss."

"Here's how I would deliver it because you know what? Three minutes is all I have.

Good afternoon. JT asked me to deliver to you several critical components of where we stand with our project now, and as you see by this slide, I have that for you today. In the time he has given me, I want to highlight the one that, quite frankly, is of the greatest concern to me. The one that indicates if we don't change our process very quickly, we stand to have a ten million dollar fine.

"Take one thing and deliver it like a superstar. Because if you get up and list twenty data points, what are you going to do?"

"Be boring," Ron answered.

"Either be boring or get trapped into rushing and throwing out data. The more that's on there, the more you rush, and what does that do to your executive presence?" He paused to let them ponder the question. "If I walked into Mizuki's office, and she told me on Monday to do that twenty point slide, you know what I might show up with? A pre-show tease slide: 'Hey, Mizuki, I have the slide you asked me to create, but I want to take a moment to show you what I think may be an opening slide to that one. I won't stay on it for more than twenty-five seconds, but it might really set the stage for what you want me to cover. Would this be okay?'"

"The worst the boss can do is say what?"

"No," Laleh answered.

"I'd go in there with a pre-show tease slide because that may be all I have to do."

"How much time should I spend on an average slide?" Ajay asked.

"I always encourage people to focus on having one key concept."

"What do you think about using music, zoom in, zoom out, animation, etc.?" Ron asked.

"Most of my corporate clients would tell you that they don't believe in a lot of bells and whistles. What I've seen work well is simple things such as the 'appear' technique. But I'd hesitate to incorporate much more than that. After all, who's the star of the show?

"Personally, I don't want technology to take over as the star. I want the slides to be the supporting cast who *reinforces* my message but doesn't *become* the message. I also don't want my audience looking for the cool stuff and missing me, the messenger."

"And it throws you off," interjected Ann. "Your style may not be a match."

"I always opt for simple slides," JT said with a shrug. "I have corporate clients who are learning to use far fewer slides, especially in the last year. Leaders are becoming much more engaged in storytelling, using key data points, and having less dependence on their slides. I believe this a really good trend because when PowerPoint is used as an aid and not a crutch, we'll get the best out of it as a tool."

Act 5: Scene I

Q&A PLACEMENT

Question 3
If you are going to include a Question and Answer (Q&A)
component as part of your presentation or meeting, it is usually best
to do so at the very end, after you finish delivering your key messages.

a. *True*

b. *False*

"This is one of my favorite questions on the quiz," JT said with a grin. "However, before we discuss the answer, let me clarify something. It is assumed that you'll be fielding questions throughout your talk. Therefore this question is referring to a defined Q&A component that you've included in your agenda.

"So what do you think, is it best to place your Q&A at the very end after you've finished delivering your key messages?"

A few of the participants murmured, "yes," fearing the answer was too obvious to say out loud.

"If you don't, won't it slow down your presentation and make you run over your time frame?" Ron asked.

"You could, but here's what I see people do all the time, Ron. Even if they've had questions in the middle, they'll say this: 'That's all I have for you today, I'd like to take our remaining time and open it up for questions.'

"I'm telling you now, don't you ever do that again. Because if you do, I am going to get on a plane, and I'm coming to get you." Turning to Andrei, he put his hand behind his ear "I can hear it now, Andrei, 'Priority Access boarding.' Come to think of it, I look good in Priority Access."

Getting back to business, he asked them, "What did you just turn over to the audience if you do what I see done all the time?"

"Command of your presentation," Ann answered.

"Yes, Ann, you've just turned over control. *I beg of you*, do not end your presentation or meeting with Q&A. Because what do we see go wrong?"

Not waiting for an answer, JT demonstrated, "You've had a few questions throughout the meeting, everything is fine. You've finished with your message so now you say, 'I'd like to see what other questions you have.' What can go wrong?" JT prodded.

"It goes off topic," David answered.

"Yes, it goes off topic, David," JT agreed. "Ron brings up something totally unrelated to your message and now, who's just ended your meeting? Ron did.

"What else can go wrong? It goes off topic, what else can happen?"

No one responded, so JT offered. "I've seen this happen. 'So that's all I have for you today. Are there any questions? *Any* questions?' JT asked again in a more desperate tone.

Into the silence, JT did his best cricket imitation.

"How awkward does it feel for everyone in the room when this happens? What happens to my facial expression if I'm not sure where to go from here?" JT looked like a man wishing he could disappear. Though they laughed, his scenario was painfully familiar.

"Or you get an employee, like Ron over here, who all of a sudden brings up something he's very upset about."

"That's usually the case," agreed Al said, causing a ripple of laughter.

"Ron, how did I know it was you?" JT teased.

"Al ratted me out," Ron threw back.

JT went on, "And now you've just let Ron's negativity end your meeting."

"So here's what I propose to you, even if you've had questions during your presentation. When you've finished your last message, you simply say this: 'Before I conclude this morning, do you have any additional questions?'"

For emphasis he repeated himself: "Before—I—conclude...are there any other questions you'd like to ask me?"

"So you're keeping the questions on topic. Right?" Al clarified.

"You are, but more importantly, you're keeping control, and you've given yourself a way to fix what goes wrong. 'Before I conclude, does anyone have any additional questions?'

"Now if someone goes off topic, what do you have the opportunity to do?"

"Get back on topic," Ann answered.

JT acknowledged Ann with a nod and then demonstrated his point. "Al, thank you for bringing a different perspective to the meeting. It would be very helpful if you and I could meet some time this week, so we can bring something back to the team on Monday.

"You now have a way to come back to you. Just as in television, you have to have some way to bring it back to the anchor before you go to commercial. Ron, the disgruntled employee brings up something negative, and now you have a way to do what?"

"Go back to your topic," Al answered.

"Exactly, Al. I am convinced that people remember what they hear at the very beginning and at the very end the most. Do you want it ending on a negative employee, do you want it ending off topic, or do you want it ending with crickets? Of course not, so now you can clean up any problem that's come up, and you're able to say: 'Seeing there are no further questions, in conclusion—point one, two, three. Our next steps are…and thank you all very much for coming to our meeting today.

"I just find it gets awfully awkward when people don't set it up with 'Before I conclude.'

"Now tell me this, and please, no one report me to either of the marketing departments. What do you typically see on a PowerPoint slide when someone goes to their question and answer time?"

"Q&A," Andrei answered, stating the obvious.

"Q&A," JT repeated, grabbing his throat, "Okay, I'm just going to scream now. I'm begging you not to do that either. Andrei, you've been talking to a group for forty-five minutes on a topic. What could be better to put on your slide instead of a question mark or the dreaded Q&A?"

"Something about the presentation?" Andrei asked, suspicious he was being set up.

"Exactly, how about displaying a quick highlight of your three key points?" JT paused to let them write the idea down as a slide popped up behind him:

Before I Conclude …
Key Message 1
Key Message 2
Key Message 3

"I have seen this work, I promise you. I talked one client team into putting their key messages back on the Q&A slide, and seventy-five percent of the questions they were asked by senior leaders came from those points. Isn't that a beautiful thing? Wouldn't it be wonderful if seventy-five percent of your questions were based on what you've just spent forty-five minutes presenting?" All were in eager agreement at the simplicity of this incredibly useful tip.

"That's control and command. Would this take you more than a minute? No."

Act 5: Scene II

Q&A MASTERY

Behind him, the next slide popped up:

Managing the Audience

"Now I'd like to give you a few tips for really nailing your Q&A," JT said. "Let me begin by asking you this: have you ever been in a meeting where you asked a question, and by the time the speaker answered it, you had no idea what they said? In fact, you could barely remember your question?"

"Oh yeah," Al said as the rest chuckled.

"Have you ever been one of those speakers?" JT teased.

"Noooo, not me," Al said, slowly shaking his head.

"Well just in case you find someone who has this problem, here's a technique to fix it."

A bullet point appeared on the screen.

- Use headline answers

"From now on, tell them to give headline answers," JT said, pointing to the screen. "A headline answer is where you tell the person exactly what they want to know first, and then you follow it up with more information if necessary.

"I'll show you what I mean. Let's say Laleh asks me if I'm going to need to add ten or eleven new people to staff my project. I respond, 'Laleh, I'll need to add eleven new people and here's why....'

"It's the opposite of what we usually see done, isn't it? Most of us tend to lead with our explanation and then answer the question. Unfortunately, by the time we get around to the answer, they're either bored, annoyed, or both.

"Please, whenever someone asks you a question—answer it even if you know they don't want to hear your answer. Nothing is gained by making someone wait and there is much to lose."

- Acknowledge the positive

"So tell me, do any of you repeat the questions people ask you?"

"Sometimes," David answered. "If I don't think other people heard it."

"I would agree with you on that point, David," JT responded. "But let me offer this idea. I would propose you repeat some of the *positive* questions you get asked if the audience is large enough to make it seem reasonable, and you want to make sure everyone is paying attention to a good question. I say this because it allows you to maintain control of the message. For instance, if Ron asks a positive question such as: 'JT, are you saying your team is going to be ready by next week?' I'm going to repeat that by saying: 'Ron wants to confirm that my team is going to be ready next week, and the answer is yes, Ron, I'm happy to report, we will be ready next week.'

"If Ron has a positive question, especially one that highlights good news, I certainly want to repeat it."

- Neutralize the negative

"Now let's say Andrei asks me a question that's negative. Do I want to repeat that? Yes, but only after I neutralize it. So Andrei asks: 'JT are you telling us that your project spent an additional five hundred thousand dollars?'

"I'm going to keep Andrei's negative emotion from entering my meeting, while still answering his question: 'Andrei has a question about the budget.'

"Do you see how this could keep your audience on track?" JT asked. Everyone was too busy writing to offer an answer. "Using tactics like this keeps you in control. It keeps you on the offensive in Q&A, rather than slipping into the defensive. After all, what does it normally feel like when we stand up and open the floor for Q&A? It feels a bit like a firing squad and you can almost feel yourself get into a defensive position as you field the questions being fired at you. Spending time planning your Q&A and employing techniques like this one assures that you are driving forward in an offensive stance… ready to win the game."

- The eyes have it…

"You know, one of the challenges I hear nearly every day is people feeling a lack of engagement with their audiences. Now, I want to begin by saying *everything* we do and say from the front of the room feeds into our ability to engage the audience. But this little tip can make a very large difference. This is another example of how the smallest changes can equal big results."

JT stepped over to face Andrei. "Our friend, Andrei here, has just asked me a question. Initially I am going to maintain eye contact with him as I start my answer. However, I don't want to lose the rest of you, so now I want to keep my eyes moving around the room as though each of you asked the question." JT demonstrated as he explained. "As I complete my answer, I will return to Andrei so I can check his body language to see if he's satisfied."

"Why do you think this might be really important? How would this help me maintain engagement?" JT stopped to ask them.

"Because you want to include everyone else," Andrei said.

"You're watching the body language of everyone to see if they're interested and if they seem to understand your point," Ann said.

"Yes, I want to include everyone, and I'm constantly checking in to see how connected they are. Yes to both of those reasons and to one more. I use this technique because I want to be sure I don't get pulled into a private conversation with this person.

"Here's the scenario. Andrei asks me a question on a topic of which I am quite knowledgeable, and it's something that interests both of us. If I'm not careful, we could end up in a one-on-one discussion that could wander off of my message and completely lose the rest of my audience.

"I've seen this happen again and again especially with technical experts. They get lost in conversation and miss an opportunity to deliver their message to everyone present. A great way to support audience engagement is to keep checking in through eye contact."

• Be confident in your answers

"Now let me ask you this, and I'll warn you right up front, it's a trick. How many of you take a question, answer it, and then go back to that person and say 'Did I answer your question?'"

Without waiting for a response, JT said, "For those of you who do, I am absolutely begging you to not ever do that again—at least not in a face-to-face meeting. Because what happens?"

"They can lead you off topic," Ann answered.

"Definitely. Lead you off topic. They can also use up your time, can't they?" JT expounded. "There you stand with a mere ten minutes, and now this intruder takes another ninety seconds, and it didn't have to be that way. It happened because you turned over control.

"To avoid this situation, begin by being absolutely clear of the question you're answering. If you have any doubts, get clarity first. Once you know the question, then answer it to your satisfaction.

"Next, rather than automatically reverting to the 'did I answer your question?' Challenge yourself to be the confident leader who can read their body language. Look at the person's face to see if you're getting neutral. If you are, then move on. If he still has questions, he can come back at you—place the responsibility onto his shoulders.

"The other problem I see along these same lines is speakers become very repetitive. 'Andrei, did I cover what you need?' 'David, are we kind of on the right path?' After a while, what does it sound like you're doing? It begins to sound like you doubt yourself. As though you're not confident enough to answer the question, so you have to check in, and what does that do to your message?"

"Kills it," Andrei said. "What about saying, 'that's a good question?'"

"You know Andrei, I would be careful of using that for three reasons." JT held up a finger. "One, it can sound very disingenuous. So many people use it as a way to stall for time that it's often hard to believe when people say it, especially if they say it repeatedly.

"Two," JT elaborated, adding a finger to make his point. "You don't want your audience thinking they've thought of something you completely missed. I've seen speakers who become so excited about a question they make it seem like the person who asked it knew more than they did about the topic. For the same reason, I sparingly use comments like, 'thank you for bringing that up.'

"Finally, three," JT said, waving three fingers in the air, "What happens when I say: 'That's a great question, Ann'; 'That's a great question, David'; 'That's a great question, Andrei.' But I don't say it when Mizuki asks a question?

"Mizuki will look at me and ask, 'What the heck, JT, am I chopped liver over here?' Not a pretty picture. For the sake of your executive presence, don't allow yourself these costly habits."

JT looked around the room and determined the group was a little restless. He dismissed them for a break, asking them to return fresh and ready to dive back into the material.[5]

---

5   Scan this QR code to discover other managing-the-audience tips.

Act 5: Scene III

DELIVERING DIFFICULT NEWS

Most of the group had used their break to step outside and breathe in the beach air. They were just settling back in when shouting suddenly erupted from the kitchen. The argument details were lost in the tirade—the expletives were not. Though startled, all assumed David and Andrei were finally locking horns, and no one moved to intercede.

"You hear that, Mr. Anderson? That is the sound of inevitability."[6] Ann murmured, citing a line from one of her favorite movies.

Then David walked into the conference room and asked if anyone knew the source of the ruckus. Instantly, they all hurried toward the sound to investigate.

What they discovered was Ron waging a verbal attack on Al— Ron's six feet six inch frame towering over Al's retracted five feet eight

---

6   This is a quote from the movie, *The Matrix*.

inches. The group's approach disrupted Ron's tirade, and Al seized the opportunity to move out of harm's way.

Ron, feeling self-conscious by his outburst, did his best to decompress. Al, miserable at what had transpired, apologized for upsetting him. Turning to address his audience that now included JT, he said, "Apparently, there is such a thing as a bad POW."

No one moved so Al went on to explain. "I wanted to practice my POW for an announcement I have to make next week. I knew this was going to be a hard thing to hear, particularly for Ron and his team. Stupidly, I thought this would be the perfect way to tell him. Again, Ron, I really am sorry."

Ron shrugged, trying to appear casual. "Don't worry about it. There wasn't any better way to tell me." He fooled no one.

"Thank you both," JT said sincerely. "You've just influenced our next discussion: How to deliver difficult news. Why don't we head back inside to delve into this challenging subject?"

Once everyone was settled, JT approached Ron and Al. "You two seem to have gotten through the worst of it. Would you be willing to share this learning moment?"

"Yeah, why not?" Ron answered glumly.

"We decided to practice our POWs with each other," AL told the group. "I thought a light-hearted approach would be a good idea. Unfortunately, it didn't work out that way."

"Al, could you please re-enact what you said?"

"Ah…sure," Al said, rising to join JT. "My POW went something like this…." The role-play brought out Al's nerves causing him to place his hands in his pockets and stare straight down at the ground. "Ah… hey, Ron, so…ah…how's the weather over your way in November? Ah…is it a good time for an OTS audit?" Immediately, Al charged back to his seat.

Ron took over the explanation. "I knew right away that Al was saying this was actually going to happen and the rest…well, the rest is what you all saw and heard."

"For the sake of clarity, will one of you please tell us what an OTS is?" JT requested.

Ron clarified. "An over-the-shoulder or OTS audit is a very invasive experience where the auditor literally stands behind the employee to observe and correct every move they make. These audits cause production slow downs, tick off employees who feel spied on, ignore the larger picture of our schedule, and…well, there are lots of reasons not to do them."

Al then took over. "We only do them in situations where there's a clear problem that needs to be addressed. We would never put any of our people through it for no reason. This time it's being federally mandated, and if we don't do the audits, we risk enormous fines." JT noticed that when Al spoke from his chair, his "ahs" and "ums" were absent.

"When you were thinking about your topic, Al, did you have another idea for a POW?" JT asked.

"Yup," Al said.

"Is it ready to deliver or do you need a minute?"

"I think it's close enough to ready. Can I do it from here?" Al pleaded.

"Al, I would never be so cruel as to make you miss a great chance to practice," JT answered with a grin. "However, I do want you to try something for me. Before you start, I want you to put your hands in front of your lower stomach area. I also want you to close your eyes and picture yourself talking to your team."

Taking a deep breath, Al began again. "Guys, we've been told by the feds that either we do OTS audits or risk costing the company millions. As we all know, fines this big could only lead to more layoffs. I know this is a pain in the ah…neck." Al's eyes opened as he grinned and shrugged at them.

He then continued with his eyes open. "Let's team up to get these rotten things done as fast as possible, and with the highest possible rating, so we can all feed our families next Christmas."

"Wow," Laleh reacted without prompting. "Al, that was so much better. Your voice was strong and clear, and your concern for your people came through really well."

"I thought that was full of executive presence," said David.

"Why?" JT asked, probing for details, "What behaviors gave you that impression?"

"I thought he came right out with the bad news and didn't pretend to sugar coat it. To me, that felt more like leadership."

"That certainly addressed the issue from the perspective of the audience. Great job," JT commented.

"By the way, do you all remember how I said you can talk about the company or anything other than yourselves? Well, I think Al just proved my point. As soon as he started talking about something he knew would be hard on his people, he became a first class spokesperson.

"As for his POW, sure, he might have had a misstep with Ron. But folks, that's why we practice. That's why I encourage you to work in teams, so you can run these past each other before you get in front of an audience." Walking to the front, JT added. "Al, you could give me difficult news any day of the week."

Al was blown away. His leadership had always felt so natural that he never gave himself much credit for his skills. Nor had anyone ever encouraged him as a speaker. Retirement was suddenly starting to seem premature.

"Just be sure you don't sound weak." Andrei instructed. "They'll take you down if you do that."

"It's critical for teams to believe we care, isn't it, Laleh? At the same time, they need to know someone is in charge and prepared to lead, don't they, Andrei? So let's talk about how to prepare ourselves, so we can cover both bases."

Stepping over to the white board, JT turned and said, "You are about to deliver a difficult message without any PowerPoint slides. What are some of the challenges you face?"

"Either they don't believe you, or they take it out on you," Al replied frankly.

"Or they know more than you do," Ron added.

"Most of the time that's true," Al agreed. "It's really difficult when the executives share something at a meeting before you've shared it with your management."

"Sure, because you feel blindsided," JT affirmed. "It's hard when you're giving bad news, and they've already got an edge on you."

"And they have more details than you do," Ron reiterated.

"Or you feel horrible about it. Like this merger," David said, shaking his head. "Anxiety and emotions," Andrei said with distaste.

"I understand you need to have facts when you're delivering, but ultimately when people get bad news, they're in a very emotional place, and you have to match emotion with emotion. It can't be all facts and figures. I always think:

Emotion + facts = caring strength

"The best kind of leader I know is one who can give the emotional connection and add the facts to it. That's a scenario that adds up to caring strength.

"Which of these is the toughest group to whom you've had to deliver bad news: your employees, your senior leaders, or your clients?" JT asked them.

"I'm not sure it's harder because of one audience or another; I think it's hard anytime there's change." Ann stated matter-of-factly. "It seems like no one really wants to accept change."

Al disagreed. "It's probably more difficult for the senior leaders knowing that they're the ones who made the decision to take that route. Whereas when we give bad news to our employees, they realize that the decision didn't come from us. It came from higher up."

"We must still take ownership," Andrei commanded. "Oh yes, I still take ownership. I'm not saying that…."

"That's like giving someone else the blame," Andrei insisted.

"I'm not saying give someone else the blame; I'm saying when it's time for layoffs, it wasn't me that made that decision to lay off ten percent of our people," Al stated defensively, his tone matching Andrei's. "It's hard when you have to deliver something you don't even believe in."

JT jumped in to shift the direction of the discussion, "A healthcare client of mine was having a strategy meeting because the very next morning they were going to announce cutbacks in employee healthcare coverage, pensions, and benefits."

"We've had to do that," Al interjected.

"You have my profound sympathy," JT said sincerely. "I wasn't brought in for their meeting; I just happened to be on-site for a coaching session. But someone saw me and asked me to help them formulate a plan. To get things rolling, I had them take me to the space where they'd be delivering the information.

"We went to the five-hundred-seat auditorium to take a look at it. It was a very tall stage with a podium. What do you think I said first?"

"Get rid of the podium," several people answered in unison.

"Yes, I said, 'don't think for a minute you're going to deliver bad news behind a podium. Not going to happen.' Because with a stage that was up really high, this is how it looked." JT bent over as though looking down on something little. "We're cutting your healthcare coverage, little people.

"You have to think about the setup of your room, even a room like this, so it doesn't become a distraction and work against you.

"The next topic of debate was how to stage the three people speaking: the CEO, CFO, and the HR manager. I asked how they were going to handle it. They said each would walk out onto the stage to present their part.

"I asked where the others would be standing while one was presenting. When they told me the others would be behind the stage curtain, I told them no.

"Why do you think I encouraged them to all be on the stage at the same time?"

"You need it to look unanimous," David said.

"You have to show a unified front. You know why? Because if you don't know the answer, perhaps your colleague does, and she can speak immediately versus you being out there all alone and caught off guard. Any time you're surprised, it can taint your executive presence and delivering bad news is hard enough when you're at your best.

"And please don't ever compare yourselves to people who make less money. One organization's top leader was to announce cutbacks in pension and benefits to his employees. Someone thought it would be good for the leader to say in his opening statement that the cuts were across the board and his family would also face struggles as a result. Wrong! I've never seen this strategy work. Never compare your situation to someone else's when they make less money. It simply doesn't work."

"So, what are some tough topics you have to share with senior leaders?"

The group flooded JT with topics.

- Performance has declined
- Deadlines not met
- Overtime budget
- Employee injury
- Bad audit
- Plant equipment damage
- OSHA violation

"What examples of bad news do you have to tell your customers?" Again the group had no trouble thinking of challenging messages.

- Delivery delays
- Employee strikes
- Price increases
- Quality issues

"Okay, let's stop there because I'm starting to get depressed," JT joked.

"Buck up, JT, this is our daily life," Ron replied.

"Okay, what topics would you have to deliver to a group of employees?"

- Merger/no merger
- Benefit changes
- More work, fewer people
- Pension discontinuation
- Contract concessions

JT pulled the flip chart page off the easel and asked who often has to speak to employees. Al raised his hand. By doing so, he became the leader of Team Employees.

"Who speaks to customers?"

Andrei reluctantly volunteered, "We'll do it."

"Great, you're our other team leader. Ajay, you're in charge of the senior leadership address."

JT then assigned the other participants to teams in order to create Massive-Cascade hybrids.

"In just a few minutes, I'm going to send you to break out rooms. Team leaders, you need have your team choose one topic around which the team feels like they can put together a message. I'm looking for these elements when you come back in here: I want a POW, and I want to hear your three key messages. You have creative license here—I'm not going to check data.

"For the third part of the assignment, I want you to think of the three toughest questions your team will be asked. You don't have to write out the answers to the questions; I just want to know the three toughest questions you think you'll be asked.

"You have twenty minutes to put together a three-minute presentation with no slides. Part of your assignment is to decide who is going to manage each part of your presentation. Is one person going to deliver one message? Three messages? Is one person going to manage the questions? You need to strategically think about how to give the best possible presentation.

"When you come back, each team will deliver their topic. The rest of us, the audience, are going to assume the role of customers, senior leaders, and employees. Be sure you remember to say, 'before we conclude,' and then open it to questions. Count on us having questions. You're going to answer the questions, you'll give us the conclusion, and then we'll give you feedback.

"The first thing I will ask when each group is finished is, 'are the questions you were asked the questions you anticipated?' There's a real key in learning to do this. There's a method to my madness with this assignment.

"One last quick suggestion, don't try to write the POW first, get your key messages down and then establish your POW. My clients find that more often than not, once their messages are clear, the POW seems obvious.

Wanting to get through the exercise as quickly as possible, David, Ron, Al and Laleh walked to the front. The four of them were a bit on edge—even Laleh was showing a slight case of nerves. Despite the fact that they were seasoned professionals, being so closely scrutinized by their peers made them all a bit jumpy.

David spoke first after taking a step forward. "Good afternoon, everyone. This is the kind of news that is never easy to announce." His rich, deep voice was an ideal match to the gravity of the situation, though his pace caused him to lose his breath. "As of this afternoon, our competition has filed a suit to block our merger. Because of that, it has just come down from HR that we are now expecting an additional ten percent in layoffs. Ron…."

Ron stepped up nervously as David retreated. "The…ah…procedure for the layoffs will be just as we've done in the past where we sit down with employee leadership and see what we can absorb by attrition…and uh…see what the net results are and…um, see…if, um…we need to do some layoffs."

After taking a deep breath to try and gather his thoughts, Ron continued. "So, we're going to anticipate more layoffs, we're going to mitigate it as much as possible, and like I said, we'll be sitting down with the leadership to see what we can do by attrition and explore any other options that are available to us at the time. Al…." Ron sighed with relief. He knew he'd gotten off to a rough start, but felt fairly confident that he'd finished strong.

Al's comfort came as a surprise to everyone…except Al. What his audience didn't know was that Al had vast experience with leading meetings to announce layoffs. While he certainly didn't enjoy it, he'd honed the skill set necessary to get through it. "Currently, there are some leading indicators that point to a thirty percent reduction initially. The thirty percent will affect all groups—so no one group will have to bear the whole burden. Also, we'll do all we can to have people move into other departments."

Being sure to make eye contact with everyone seated, he continued. "Right now, we don't have any information regarding the dates these changes will be effective. However, we anticipate we'll have an initial outlay by the third quarter. Laleh…."

Once again proving to be a "people person," Laleh stepped up and spoke in a tone filled with care and concern. "Because we know the process is so difficult for our people, we have plans in motion now to ensure we provide a maximum amount of support and information. Number one: we're going to provide bi-weekly updates to tell you as much as we know as soon as we know it. Second, we're going to provide support for those who are affected. We're partnering with local and state agencies to provide alternative employment opportunities. Finally, we will provide education in job placement skills such as resume writing and interview tips. Before we conclude, are there any questions?"

After fielding several pertinent questions, the role-play came to an end. The audience clapped enthusiastically, while JT stepped to the front. "Feedback, please," he instructed.

"Everyone had a very good part to play in it," Ann observed. "All of them had good body language, and they all sounded very convincing and confident about what they were discussing. They had very natural transitions as they handed off to the next speaker, without it seeming overly staged. It was very free flowing."

"Very cohesive," JT agreed. "How was the POW, using a statistic?"

"Great," Ajay answered, stepping out of his usual silence.

"If I were to have you do anything, it would be to slow down just slightly, so I could take in each one of those sentences. I thought they were very powerful. I'd just like a chance to process them, that's all," JT commented.

Addressing everyone, he said, "We all need to remember that if we're leading the discussion, it means we've had a chance to think it over and more than likely our audience has not. It's critical that we not move too fast, so they can absorb the news."

"Anything else?" JT paused before asking. "Did it feel different to step into being the speaker?"

"Yes." They responded.

"It helps us focus as an audience when we know who's speaking, doesn't it? It feeds the cohesiveness.

"A suggestion for this team and for everyone in this room: when you have difficult news to deliver, you want to incorporate the actual use of time. It's the one thing that I didn't hear from anyone. For example, I might say, 'Ron, this Friday, we're meeting with the leadership to decide our three proactive strategies. We plan to meet with Al and his team next week to present. We're on their calendar for next Thursday.

"When we can use time elements…what sense does it create in the audience?" JT asked. He then answered, "Assurance and a sense of urgency that you're being proactive. So, I always tell people when you've got to give bad news, use time frames. Don't say we're going to have a meeting, say: 'We're going to meet Friday, ten o'clock, at headquarters to talk about….'

"It says so much. You're already doing it; you might as well be clear about what you're doing.

"Another takeaway from this exercise is how often we go in to deliver bad news without getting any input from our team. I realize there isn't always time. But listen, I gave you twenty-five minutes and wasn't it useful that you had people to help you brainstorm? We don't do enough of that in the real world. It can't always work out, but if you have to go in at four o'clock and give some bad news, can't you say, 'Andrei do you have five minutes today? I have a tough message to deliver at four. I just want to brainstorm and run it by you to get your perspective.'

"I can tell you that you'll be better at four o'clock because you did that with him for five minutes. It works because, in essence, you've just done a dress rehearsal. It lets you run through your entire message one time before you go in front of an audience, and it lets you get some honest feedback. I think we don't get enough of that in the real world."

Ann jumped in. "I think it's difficult to present with three, four, or five people. Doing it alone is hard, but with four other people, it's even harder to find the cadence of your delivery."

"Normally we don't do that," Al agreed. "It's either one or two at max, and most of the time, you're asked to do a project on your own, especially when it comes to presentations. So when you're doing it with a group of people, it's awkward."

"Yet, look what you did in twenty-five minutes," JT encouraged them to consider.

Ann agreed, "I know, I thought it was great."

"It looked really good," JT agreed with Ann, glad to see she was continuing to warm up. "It was incredibly cohesive, and I would propose to you that if there were two hundred fifty people in that audience, I'd prefer to like see three or four leaders up there. I think it gives a unified front."

"We don't consider that because typically in a message like this, HR will be right up there with you. They answer the questions much better than we can," Ron said.

"Fair enough, Ron." JT responded. "The point of this is to give you options."

"Yeah," Ron agreed with a nod, "I can see this being really useful in some cases."

"Another thing I would share with you that I find to work in a crisis scenario, especially when you have little time to prepare is to think about the three Cs. They are:

Control—Concern—Cooperation

"You don't have to use these three words, but I think they are very helpful in a crisis.

"First is control—when people are in crisis mode they want to know what? They want to know that you've got it under control. They want to know that you're dealing with the issue, you're tackling it, and you've got it under control. And if you don't have it under control, tell them what you are doing to get it that way.

"Next—they want to know it is of great concern to you. That it matters to you, that you're passionate and empathetic.

"And finally, they want to feel a sense that you're cooperating with the union leaders, that you're cooperating with OSHA, whatever it might be. When you can think in terms of these three words and when you have a little time to prepare, these are three very good safeguards to use: in control, of great concern, in cooperation with all agencies involved.

"This is easy for me to say standing here, yet I realize you're the ones that have to actually do this. But let me ask you, when you can stay calm and in control, that really kills some of them in that audience, doesn't it? Because they want to get you; they want you to lose it," JT said.

Al agreed. "That happened to me once, though it was probably only a few—say three out of twenty who did it. But I knew if I went back at them, they would just feed on it. I also knew the rest of the people were watching me and how I reacted to the situation."

"That's exactly what I've seen happen, too, Al," JT agreed. "There are those who attack and those who observe. My approach is to realize that I'm probably not going to change those three you mentioned, no matter what. But I still have the other seventeen people I may be able to influence in a positive way."

"And those seventeen people probably gained a lot of respect just watching you refrain," Al interjected.

"That's right, Al. You know, I'm not going to get a one hundred percent, or in your case, twenty-to-zero vote of confidence. But, if I can get a seventeen-to-three vote of confidence…it doesn't get any better than that. I probably can't do anything with those three anyway."

"Why did you have us think of three questions and answer them before we were asked?" Ann asked.

"For our big presentations, we often get so busy creating PowerPoint slides that we forget to stop and think about the three toughest questions those people are going to ask. Despite how important it is, we don't take the time to prepare our answers," JT answered. "The reason I like to do this exercise is to show you the value of taking the time to do so."

Laleh reflected, "One of the key things I liked about this exercise was asking myself the questions I thought I might be asked. It provided me with a direction for the content. I thought that was extremely powerful."

"Going a step further—here you have your three questions. You look at question two, and you know good and well it's going to be asked."

"Just say it," Ann interjected.

"Exactly, Ann, make it one of your three messages. Why wait? Because once you go to Q&A it's harder to stay in control. Once it goes to Q&A, you've lost an edge. If you know question two is going to come up, deal with it and make it one of your key messages. If you know it's going to be prevalent on their minds, I think it says you thought about your audience. It's another way to *know* your audience. By the way, you'll also want to prepare answers for the easiest questions that may be asked. Campaigns have been lost on the question, 'why do you want to be president?'"

Act 6: Scene I

THE ORDER OF THINGS

Question 4
*If you're giving a presentation using PowerPoint and a key
stakeholder asks a question related to something you know is on
slide five, and you're on slide two, what should you do?*

*a. Tell the person you'll get to that information/answer in
just few more slides*
b. Tell the person you'll take questions at the end
*c. Answer the question immediately, either with or
without going to slide 5*

"**C**," they sang out. The now-familiar red circle confirmed their answer.

"Ajay, I wrote this question because a senior executive told me to put this question on the quiz. He said to me, 'JT, if I ask a question, I don't ever want to be told to 'hold that thought' because the information is coming up in a couple of slides. Nobody better ever tell me that. When I ask a question, I expect it to be answered.'

"That's why I'm saying answer immediately—with or without going to the corresponding slide. Here it becomes a difficult balancing act because if I go to slide five what have I turned over? I've turned over control. So ideally, I don't want to go there.

"I'm going to propose this to you. When a leader has asked you a question, try to give him or her what we call in television the pre-show tease. For instance: 'Coming up tonight on Tulsa news—our top stories.'

"They do that at 5:59, and thirty seconds before the six o'clock news show starts to get you to do what?"

"To watch," they answered simultaneously.

"To watch and not turn over to another channel…and that's what you have to do. For example:

Ajay, in the Massive employee opinion survey, eighty-five percent of our employees felt we were doing a better job as a management team with our communications skills. That's up ten percentage points from last year when it was seventy-five percent. Throughout the presentation, I would like to share with everyone how our employees ranked us in different categories. It was certainly a plus to go up ten percentage points.

"That was the pre-show tease. The pre-show tease works well when you can give them what? One data point." Turning back to Ajay, JT emphasized, "Eighty-five percent of our employees felt we were doing a better job communicating to them.

"Because when you can give them one data point, what does that tell that one person and the audience?"

"You know your material," Andrei answered.

"You know your material," JT repeated. "And I think you have a better chance of holding them off. Because there was something concrete in there. It didn't sound like a fluff answer.

"Also, when you get to slide five you still have some relevant data to share that you haven't already presented," Ajay added.

"Absolutely," JT agreed.

"Ajay, to your question earlier, you'll see that it's at eighty-five percent, but I'd like to draw your attention to their responses about inclusiveness.

"And now you've stayed in control because you didn't have to go to slide five. So, the pre-show tease with one data point, if it exists, is how you stay in control. However, what if there is something on that slide that is just critical to what you've just been asked? You simply have to go there. So I go to five, I answer the question, I show him the graph, and then what do most people do?"

"They go back," Andrei stated, confident it was the right move.

"This same senior executive said to me, 'JT, couldn't they challenge themselves just to go forward? Was there really anything on slides three and four they couldn't just tell me?'

"Because when you go back, what happens? It's awkward, isn't it?' I thought that was a fair point."

"You appreciate the flexibility in somebody if they can. At least I appreciate it," Ann interjected.

"And normally by asking you the question about what's on page five it's essentially their way of telling you, 'I got it. I get what's in three and four,'" Laleh added.

"The other thing that happens is it may be telling you that you have too much in your presentation for that type of audience. We often hear 'get that down to three slides,'" Al added.

"In order to be able to skip around through slides, you really have to be prepared and know your presentation," David said solemnly. "It's usually not a situation where you can just wander around."

"Right. There is no substitute for preparation, is there?" Both men shook their heads in agreement.

Act 6: Scene II

THE POWER OF THREE

"**H**ere's what I'd like you to take from this question. If I am on slide two and a senior leader gives me a question from slide five, what does that infer about the order of my presentation?"

"That the presentation needs to be re-organized," Ann replied.

"Exactly, Ann. Thank you," JT said with a smile. "Clearly I did not have what mattered to him up front, and therefore, I have made an error in the organization of my presentation. Here's where the trouble starts, it begins with people wanting to talk in chronological order."

On the flip chart, JT wrote:

$$A + B = C$$

"This is how it goes: 'Good morning, everyone. Thank you for coming to our staff meeting. Today, I want to give you an update on where we stand on this engine initiative. First, I want to share with you where we've been the last six weeks and some of the things we've accomplished. Next, I want to share with you where we are today. Finally, I want to share with you what we're going to do in the next six weeks, which is quite frankly, going to transform the way we do business here at Massive.'

"What was the most interesting of those three?"

"Transform," Mizuki responded.

"That's right—C is the future. It's the good stuff, and yet, many of us take twenty minutes to get to the good stuff and by the time we do, they are bored out of their minds. I don't think you can afford to present in chronological order. I think you have to give your audience information in compelling order. So, this is really a better equation:

$$C = A + B = C$$

"There may be rare times when A + B = C is best, for example when C is controversial, you may need to ease them into it. I'll give you that. But most of the time, I see people using chronological order when they should be doing compelling order. You have to put what matters to that audience up front.

"Now, let me ask you this, have any of you ever been in a scenario where you knew you had twenty minutes, but when you walked in the door someone in upper management told you, 'We know we told you twenty minutes but now you have five.'

"We've all had that happen. We've all heard 'could you cut it to five?' If you follow my model, this C is your five minutes. Now, instead of trying to jam a twenty-minute presentation into a five-minute time slot, a tactic that never works by the way, you have five minutes of powerful messaging."

"So let's say you go to slide five and answer the question," Ron posed. "You're suggesting we move forward. But what about the rest of the audience, what if they could be interested in what's on slides two, three, and four? Maybe they're not concerned about the guy who wants to see slide five, and now you've just moved forward. What if they see it as you just kind of blowing them off?"

With an impatient sigh, Andrei responded, "It's determined by what's on slides two, three, and four, and how pertinent it is that you have to show the information."

"I think this comes down to reading the body language. Right?" JT interceded. "Really seeing and getting a feel for where they are. If you've got a lot of people nodding, you're probably okay to move on. If you look around and you have a lot of dazed looks, then either you have to talk your way through those skipped slides, or you may have to go back." Making sure they all heard his point, he reiterated. "I'm not saying *never* go back, but you have to be savvy enough to read the audience to know what to do. I'm simply saying consider your options and avoid going back if you can.

"My point is to make sure we've answered the question in a way that allows the person who asked it to be satisfied. This is absolutely critical if it's a decision maker because we want to be sure they're listening to the rest of the presentation.

"While we're on the subject of getting the order right, let's talk about how to lay out your presentation." Raising his hand, JT asked, "How many of you read the meeting invites you receive?" No one mirrored his pose.

"I just don't have the time. There are too many of them," Al responded.

"That's exactly what all of my clients say, and that's why I'm a big fan of having an agenda slide. It doesn't need to take long, a mere fifteen seconds in many cases. The key is to make sure they know why they're there. Of course, this is after your POW.

"Once you've covered your agenda, it's time to present your *three* key messages. *Only three*. Even if you have seven different topics, your most effective strategy is to arrange those topics into three categories. Why? Because every study tells us that people remember in threes, and therefore, your audience can't walk away with seven.

"Let's look at this from a marketing perspective: How many stooges are there?"

"Three," they all answered with a laugh.

"Rice Krispies has how many animated spokesmen?"

"Three," they answered again.

"Snap, Crackle, and..." Al said, trying to remember. "Pop," David added, lending him a hand.

"The show from the '70s with Fred MacMurray had how many sons? "Three."

"For those of you who live anywhere near a Pep Boys franchise? How many pep boys are there?"

"Three." The chorus continued.

"Manny, Mo, and Jack," Al said, pointing to David to prove this time he was sure.

"Companies do this because marketing experts know there's something memorable about the number three. Now put those three points into compelling order as we've just discussed, and you'll be amazed at how effective your presentations will be.

"You're going to want to write down this next point. If you're half asleep, wake up and hear me on this one. Bring in an outside source. Every presentation should have one outside source: a data point, a statistic, or a quote: some piece of information that is not from Massive or Cascade. Why do you think that is? When you bring in an outside source, what does it tell your audience that you did?"

"Research," Andrei answered.

"Yes, Andrei, it tells them you did your research," JT agreed. "You know, I get pushed back on this one from clients who tell me they don't have time for research. But I say this: Give me five minutes and access to Google, and I'll find a valuable outside source on virtually any topic. Can you think of a more valuable use of five minutes when preparing your pitch?

"But now I'm going to take it one step further. What else does it say to your audience? You've now brought in this competitor's data point or an industry vision of the world for the next ten years. When you do that what does it say to your audience?"

"Confirmation," Andrei said.

"Could be confirmation of your points. However, I think it goes even beyond that, Andrei. I think it tells your audience that you're a visionary, a strategist, and that you're a big picture thinker because you can think beyond the four walls of this company. You can see how it relates to the industry. You can see the comparison of growth projections of us versus the competitors. It adds credibility. It means you don't have to take my word for it."

JT paused. "All of that return for a five-minute investment. It sure seems worth it to me."

Act 7: Scene I

"I DON'T KNOW"

Question 5
In order to protect your credibility, how many times in a
typical presentation or meeting can you tell questioners you'll
get back to them because you're just not sure at that moment?

a. 1-2
b. 3-4
c. There is no limit
d. None of these

This time instead of a chorus, the group responded with a cacophony of mumbled answers, except for Ron. He answered "C" loudly, with absolute certainty.

"Ron, could you expound on why you answered C?"

"Sure, it's because you can't lie…I've, ah, I've had some experience with this one."

JT remained silent, encouraging Ron to continue speaking as he waded through the uncomfortable memory.

"I didn't set out to lie…it's just that I panicked. I felt like I was losing ground, and there was this one guy who just kept pounding on me. So, somewhere in the middle of everything I started making up my answers." Ron's head dropped while his hand rose to cover his mouth as he spoke. "Not my shiniest moment."

JT knew Ron and everyone else was knee-deep in a powerful learning opportunity—*if* Ron was willing to open up completely.

"Ron, any chance you found yourself getting angry as the situation deteriorated?"

"Definitely. In fact, the more smoke and mirrors I tried to use, the more defensive I got. It was just a train wreck."

"Thank you so much for sharing, Ron. Allowing others to learn through your difficult experience is an extraordinary gift."

In a final act of humility, Ron admitted, "Well, I'm glad somebody can benefit from it since I'm pretty sure that meeting has stalled out my career."

A compassionate hush settled over the group. This was the first time anyone remembered seeing Ron vulnerable. Those that knew him well waited in silence, sure he'd follow up with some cynical remark. They were then doubly surprised when Ron remained quiet, allowing his vulnerability to be exposed.

"Well, you're certainly not alone in that experience," David assured him. "I know I've blown some smoke in my day. Especially when the pressure's on, it can be so tempting to reach beyond your expertise."

Ron raised his head to give David a grateful smile.

"Is C the answer?" Andrei demanded.

"Actually, it's A, though give yourself credit for whichever one you chose.'" JT answered triggering the red circle on the screen. "Please, *hear me*, I am not suggesting that you lie. I hear renditions of Ron's story in almost every session I lead, and I completely agree with Ron when he says going outside of your knowledge can have painful ramifications.

"However, I would caution you about saying 'I don't know' more than one or two times per meeting. Because when you say it more than one or two times, what does your audience begin thinking about you?"

"That you're wasting their time," Andrei said with conviction.

JT acknowledged Andrei's comment with a nod. "They're thinking, 'If you don't have your act together, why don't you come back next Thursday and try this again.' Right?"

"No...they won't give you another chance," Ron said.

"That, my friend, is unlikely. However, you will need a strategy." Walking over to the distraught Ron, JT said, "In just a few minutes we'll be discussing strategies for getting past a professional faux pas—we do this because they're such a common occurrence. I assure you, Ron, if you're willing to stick to a strategy, you'll see a way to get your career back on track." For the first time in months, Ron's eyes held a glimmer of hope.

Heading back to the front of the room, JT returned to the topic at hand. "So, we're all in agreement that there's no limit to being truthful. If you don't know, you don't know. But I often find people say 'I don't know' before they need to say it. And believe me, there are many *better* ways that you can buy yourself a little time.

"Imagine we're all in a meeting, and I've already said 'I don't know' twice. Ann has just asked me a question, and *again* I don't have the answer. What are some things I might do before I say 'I don't know' for a third time?"

"BS!" Ron offered with a Cheshire grin. "Isn't that what we're here to learn?"

"You've been waiting for quite a while to say that haven't you, Ron?" JT asked with a chuckle. "I'm glad I could help you get that off your chest."

"Go on a break," Al chimed in.

"Ask the audience," Ann offered seriously.

"You could do that, Ann. It can be a great technique, though it's certainly not without some risk. I think *one time* you could say something like:

> Thank you for bringing that question to the table, Ann. I'd like to take two minutes and get a feel for the room. What do all of you think? How might that play into our process change here?

"That's just so you can sound like you already know the answer, and now you're just asking to see if everybody else does too," Al said cynically.

"It's engaging the audience," Ann stated, slightly defensive.

"Especially if you had team members in the audience that *may* have the answer," David observed. He remained concerned about his feedback after his previous encounter with Ann and was glad to have a chance to be on her side of anything.

"It's true, isn't it? That's a good way to engage someone without throwing him or her under the bus. Now, once an audience member offers a reasonable answer, all I have left to do is wrap it up:

> I hope that was helpful for you, Ajay. Ron, I especially liked your point about the matrix environment and how we have to change that....

"I may have had no idea what Ann was asking me, but you never knew it."

"You'll see a lot of CEOs do that. Especially at big conferences," David added.

"And I appreciate that…." Ann interrupted.

"Yeah, you'll see Tom or somebody say 'Where's so and so?' as he looks out at the audience," Al recalled.

"Or 'Susan, help me out here,'" Ann added.

"And then you have to wrap it up at the end, like you said. But that's fine with me, I don't expect them to know it all," David concluded.

"Please remember all of the things we're talking about here are one-time use only; you can't do any of them more than one time per meeting. So once you've used up your free 'ask the audience' pass, what else can you do?"

"I think sometimes this is driven by my own need to be precise," Ajay ventured. "But, if I don't have the exact answer then I feel required to respond by saying, 'I'll get back to you.' Whereas perhaps I could say, 'I don't have the exact figures, but my recollection is in this range.' It is possible that will satisfy the questioner."

"Ajay, I call that type of answer taking it to the big picture. For example:

Laleh, I don't remember the exact percentage, and I will certainly get that to you as quickly as possible. But may I share with you what I saw as I looked at the overall process? It was really amazing to me that we've had a fundamental shift change.

"I didn't know the exact minute detail, but I knew the impact of the detail. Go to the big picture. Acknowledge that you don't know, tell her you'll get it, and go to the big picture.

"I think one time in a meeting you can also say:

Ann, may I ask you to repeat the question? I want to make sure that I'm following correctly.

"I think you can ask for a repeat once, especially if her question was long and possibly all over the place. What are you going to get the second time around?"

"A more condensed question," Laleh volunteered.

"Yes, I think you get a better, clearer question because some of that may have been political grandstanding on her part, or she may have been trying to share something that upset her. I think you get a better question and you buy yourself more time in front of the room or at the table.

"I also think you can do this one time:

Al, could you give us a specific example related to your question? I think it might be helpful for all of us to process. Perhaps there's some additional context.

"I think you can throw it back on them once. Now, Al might say, 'no, answer the question.' But most of the time, I think they'll give you an example. What else can you do?"

"Phone a friend," Al joked. "Take it off line," Ron added.

"I thank you for the set-up, Ron. 'If we could, let's take this off line.'"

"Or, 'Let's put that in the parking lot,'" Al interjected. Everyone nodded in agreement.

JT pretended to stick his finger down his throat. "I think those are the most over-used lines I've ever heard of in my life. Quit using them, please."

"It is better for you to say this, again, only once:

Ron, I'd like to follow up with you on that answer because I
have some exact data points back in my office. I'll send you
an email by three o'clock this afternoon.

"Doesn't that sound so much better than 'off line'? When people
hear the word 'off line' today, what do they think?"

"There's some secret," Ron answered.

"Something's secret, something's wrong, something's controversial,
or they think you just brushed off the person asking the question. They
assume you're never going to get back to that person; that was just your
way to shut them up. However, you know when I have used that line?
When the answer was going to embarrass the heck out of someone."

"Or it's going to take too long to answer it," Andrei said.

"One of the most useful ways to eliminate the idea that you're just
shutting someone up is to use time elements. Try out these examples:

We haven't addressed that issue yet, though we are
anticipating the data will become available in the next ten
days. I will be sure you receive it as quickly as possible.

Or,

I have that information back at my desk and will provide it for
you directly after this meeting.

Or,

I appreciate your bringing that up. I will do the necessary
research and have an answer for you by the end of the week.

"Can you see the power of using different language and adding a time element?" JT asked them.

"I'll get back to you on that first thing tomorrow morning," Ron answered with a chuckle.

Act 7: Scene II

BRAND REPAIR

"Now as promised, let's have a conversation about what to do when something has caused harm to our executive brand. Ron, I know you might feel alone in this situation, but I can assure you, you're not. I've had numerous clients ask me this past year...'what do I do when my brand has been damaged...a project didn't go well...I didn't make my numbers?'

"As you heard me say a few minutes ago, I believe brand repair is all about having a solid strategy. So let's run through the steps for recovering your brand. Now, before you do anything else, please check in with someone you trust to be sure that your perspective is on point. In other words, it never hurts to verify you're not making a mountain out of a molehill.

"So now, let's say it has been confirmed that there's a problem. What do you do next in a situation like that? What's your next action?" JT asked.

"Apologize," Laleh answered. The rest nodded their agreement.

"An apology is definitely a good idea, Laleh; however, I'd say there's another step that comes before the apology." Addressing the group, he asked, "What often happens if you apologize immediately without first acknowledging what went wrong?"

"I don't believe you," Ann said bitterly, inadvertently making the conversation personal.

"Why not, Ann?"

"Because 'I'm sorry' means *nothing* unless I *know* you understand the inconvenience or pain you've caused me," her jaw tightened as she spoke. "Otherwise, I have no reason to trust you won't do it again," Ann added.

"That's it, isn't it?" JT's voice acted as a softening agent to Ann's tension. "If we don't believe the person fully recognizes the damage he or she has caused, we may not be able to accept their apology and move on. We may feel unable to find any way of trusting him or her again." JT paused as Ann exhaled. Clearly, she'd waited a long time for someone to understand how she felt.

"In our personal lives, that may mean a lost relationship. At the office, that situation could result in missing out on new projects, raises, or promotions. It's a very important step.

"Once you've completed the acknowledgement, it's time to make a sincere apology. You can't forgive yourself until you've asked for forgiveness from others."

Stepping up to the white board he wrote:

Step One: Damage Control
Acknowledge what went wrong
Apologize
Be Quiet

There was a twitter of laughter when they saw he'd written "Be Quiet."

"I am absolutely serious about this," JT said in a voice that stopped them in their tracks. "You must become quiet once you've apologized. Because what happens if we keep talking about it?"

"They never forget," Ron said, realizing the role he was playing in his own demise.

"Right. Don't go on and on about it. Face it, deal with it, and then move forward."

JT stepped back up to the white board:

Step Two: Replace the Story
Gather Champions & Cheerleaders

"Find others to be your champions and cheerleaders. Your credibility has been damaged, so it will come across as 'self-serving' if you tout your accomplishments and successes immediately after your failure. Let your supporters sing your praises. They can help you restore your brand while also helping you re-gain your self-confidence."

He wrote the last step:

Step Three: Take Small Risks
Take on small projects/assignments

"Take on small projects/assignments and have a series of small wins. Don't take on a huge project—the risk is too great that you might fail again. Your credibility will be restored over time with consistent, small successes. This can be the most difficult step for many people because often, we want to do one great thing in hopes that the past will be forgotten. It's better to restore your brand over time."[7]

7   If you'd like some assistance with rebuilding your brand please click on this link or scan this QR code.

Act 8: Scene I

OPPOSING VIEWS

Question 6

If you know you're going to have an "opposer" in your presentation or meeting, it is best to acknowledge it upfront and let the "opposer" share his/her perspective before launching into your message.

a. True

b. False

"Let's start by defining what an opposer is."

"Obviously, it's Ajay," Al declared with a laugh.

"Thank you for that, Al. You know I don't want to point fingers here, but could someone hand Al a mirror?"

"I'm going to ignore that remark until after I get my lottery prize," Al retorted.

"Good decision, Al," JT said with a smile.

"I assume an opposer is someone who disagrees with your opinion," Laleh ventured.

"Exactly, Laleh. So should you invite an opposer to share their view first?"

"My initial thought was to approach them prior to the meeting to see if there's a way to agree to disagree," Laleh shared.

"No doubt, Laleh. Making a pre-emptive strike is absolutely the ideal solution. But as we all know, that doesn't always work. So then what can you do?"

"Well, I don't want them to derail my message, so I'd rather they speak their peace," Laleh answered.

"I see your point, but I wonder how many opposers can actually be trusted to quickly state their case and then turn the floor back to you?" JT posed. "Personally, I would never risk giving the floor to my opposition if it were my meeting or presentation.

"But that being said, how do you deal with the opposer in the room? How do you manage them when you've done everything you could prior to that meeting to deal with them? Yet, you *know* that two minutes into your meeting, they are going to raise their hand and start trouble."

"You could blind them with a laser pointer," Al said. JT just shook his head.

"The approach *I* find most effective is to identify the situation before anyone else can take over. Let's say Al and I are on opposite sides of an argument, and I know he's gunning for me in our meeting. I don't want to call him out, as that's just going to embarrass him, and it will likely fuel his fire."

"Bring it on," Al poked.

"But *clearly* I want to neutralize him before he has a chance to take control. For example:

I'll begin by saying our team has had some very spirited conversations about this project, and as of today, we're still in a state of disagreement. What I'd like to do is present my approach and allow the others to present their cases either later today or schedule a second meeting.

"Now what happens if Al comes after me?"

"We could throw things," Ron proposed.

Everyone laughed, "All right, let's not send anyone to the hospital, Ron," JT said with mock-exasperation. "But, your willingness to defend me from the opposer is exactly what happens when an opposer tries to attack after they've been acknowledged." Ron stood to take a bow.

"And, that's why we want to name the conflict before it erupts and costs you command and control."

"What if the opposer is just someone who doesn't agree with your opinion?" Ann asked mildly.

"Thank you, Ann. It's true, innovation requires us to make room for dissenting opinions, doesn't it?

"Therefore, we need to distinguish the different types of opposer. The first is a sane person with a rational argument for their perspective. When they argue their point, they're arguing because they believe they're right. They aren't doing it just to cause trouble. Though you still don't want them using your presentation time, at least they're the type of people with whom you can agree to disagree.

"The other type of opposer is what a client of mine calls a C.A.V.E. person—a Citizen Against Virtually Everything. These are the people who ignore the merits of a discussion and even what's best for the company, all in the name of the fight. Their goal is to win at all costs.

"C.A.V.E. people will fight to gain control for sport. They'll change sides if they sense they're losing an argument. They'll fight to the death over every issue, even if it doesn't involve them. These are the people who will do everything they can to influence others—sometimes even acting unethically just to get the win. Sound familiar to anyone?"

"Sounds a lot like Richard in quality control," Ron said to Ann, causing her to laugh out loud.

"What do you do about it?" JT asked them.

"I still have my laser pointer," Al offered.

"Keep it handy, Al, but let's consider some other ideas instead. So we have a C.A.V.E. person coming straight at us. What happens if we decide to engage in a brawl?"

"You lose," Ann replied.

"Why do you say that, Ann?"

"Because you sink to their level."

"Yes, and the audience won't come to your defense. They'll send someone out for popcorn, won't they?" They all nodded their agreement. "Do your best to stay out of their resistance.

"Now let's say you have a decision-maker that is causing the problem. What do you do?"

"Wrap it up as fast as you can?" Ajay answered with a question.

"Yes, that's one way." JT affirmed. "Another option would be to go to the black screen and just stop your presentation like this:

> Ajay, I'm concerned that my presentation isn't hitting on the information you wanted to walk away with from this meeting. Why don't we just talk it through?

"However, let's say the problem person is a member of your team and their behavior has grown consistently worse. Now what do you do?"

"Fire them," Al said with assurance.

"I understand your instincts, but for this example, we'll say that's not an option. Here's what I would suggest. First of all, I would never address someone from across the room because that brings everyone into the conversation. If this person wants to incite a riot, that is a way to make it easier for them.

"I'm going to walk over to them in a non-aggressive manner and bring the conversation down to just the two of us by dropping my volume and tone of voice like this," JT said, acting out his conversation with Andrei.

> "You know, Andrei, I hear your passion about this topic and it's clear you feel strongly about your point of view. What I need from you is a full report on your position so that the two of us can meet privately to review each point. I'll look for that report to be on my desk by four o'clock tomorrow.

"As you finish your last few sentences, begin to trail off and make eye contact with others in the room. Let the room know you're ready to move on to another question or issue."

JT added, "I had a client who went through this program, and a few days later he called to tell me it didn't work. He began by saying he'd done exactly what I'd said to do: He walked up to the C.A.V.E. man during a meeting, spoke to him one-on-one, told him to write a report, and then walked away without looking back. However, the C.A.V.E. person still came after him. At first he was annoyed with me, thinking the technique had little value. But then he received three emails from his team thanking him for finally doing something to address the problem.

"I recently saw an article that stated the most expensive employee isn't the one who is disengaged in their job. It's the employee who is negatively engaged and spends his or her days wandering the halls infecting others with their poor attitudes. Never let an opposer steal your executive presence."

Act 9: Scene I

STAND UP FOR YOUR MESSAGE

Question 7
Your voice projects better when you are standing or sitting?

a. Standing
b. Sitting

"**S**tanding," the chorus rang out.

"So tell me this, you're on a major conference call. It's an hour long, and thirty minutes into it, it's your time to talk. Are you standing for your five minutes or are you sitting?"

"Sitting," they all agreed.

"If you were sitting, get up. Just get up. You have so little you can do to make a conference call better, you should at least have a great voice. Your voice is much stronger when you're standing because what's happening? Movement. When you have physical movement, you get modulation. When you are seated in that chair for thirty minutes, guess what happens to your voice? It flat lines. It may be loud enough, but it becomes very even, very flat because you have been still for thirty minutes. Stand up.

"What if you're standing, and someone hits you with a tough question? Can I tell you I think you'll handle the question better standing? Yes, I can. People think better on their feet than from their seat.

"Now, this means there is one drawback we have to face. Here's your speakerphone or your poly-com, whatever, and now you're standing. You're too far away from the microphone. So what do I encourage all my clients to do? Spend fifty dollars, and get a headset.

"Anytime you're on a speaker and someone picks up the receiver, don't you always think 'oh thank goodness, that's so much better'? Of course, because where is the microphone now?" JT asked pointing to the short distance between an imaginary handset and his mouth.

"So, for my five minutes I would stand up, and I would wear a headset or I would pick up the phone."

"JT," Mizuki began, "if you're in a face-to-face meeting and everyone is sitting, including you, is it ever appropriate to stand up and walk around the room?"

"I think it's hard to stand up without purpose." JT grabbed a chair and sat down to demonstrate. "Let's say you've just finished your presentation seated, and now you're going into a Q&A that you know is going to be contentious. Wouldn't it be better if you could stand up?" JT paused as they nodded their agreement.

"He or she who is standing, has a better chance at control. But… you can't just finish your presentation seated and then do this." JT stood as he said combatively, "What questions do you have?"

They all chuckled.

"But I think you could do this…

I want to stop at this point before we wrap up and take any questions you might have. I realize there might be some points I'll need to follow up on, so I'd like to get to the flip chart and make some notes. This will help me later. Who had a question?

"This is the way you stand up—when you do it with purpose. You can't just stand up for no reason; it will look defensive."

Act 9: Scene II

ENGAGING CONFERENCE CALLS

"I'd like you all to take a moment to think of a fact about yourself that we would not find on your resume. Next, place your hand out on the table in front of you, palm down. As I go around the room sporadically, I'll be lightly tapping you twice on the hand. That will be my signal for you to share your fact with the group. Before we start, I'll need you all to close your eyes."

They were surprised by the exercise instructions, but at this point, they trusted JT and did what he asked without resistance. Tapping on their hands one by one, each of them shared a detail from their life story.

"I have an obsession with commercial aquariums," one of the participants said. "I love spending time sitting next to a giant tank and imagining myself swimming around the locals." They all smiled at the image.

"I'm a fisherman. From the time I was old enough to hold onto the bait, my dad and I would go out in our little boat, wet a line, and talk about guy stuff." Once again everyone enjoyed the imagery.

"I restore old cars. Every Saturday that I'm not working, I'm wrenching away on a muscle car in my garage." The last participant to share volunteered.

"Thank you," JT said. "You may all open your eyes."

"So tell me, what was this experience like?"

"I thought it was really interesting," Laleh offered. "I was never sure who was going to speak next and couldn't wait to hear what the next person might say."

"Did it affect the way you listened?" JT inquired.

"Yes, it did," she answered. "I paid a lot more attention to everyone's information."

"This exercise took less than two minutes—total. Do you think it might be an effective way to launch a conference call? Do you think you might set an entirely different tone by kicking off your call with a few human connections?"

"Yes," Laleh responded enthusiastically.

"What about the different voices?" JT inquired. "Was it intriguing to have different voices sharing?"

"I thought so," Ann answered.

"So there's another tip for you—whenever you're hosting a conference call, do your best to change voices *at least* every ten minutes or more. The fact of the matter is that no one's voice remains interesting after ten straight minutes. And as we all know, the less interested the audience is, the more multi-tasking goes on behind the scenes. What else? Everyone feel free to contribute," he invited.

"By closing my eyes, I found myself really tuned in to everyone else," David said. Ducking his head slightly, he added, "I hate to admit it, but that level of focus is unusual for me."

"Thank you, David. I appreciate your candor. I'm sure all of us can point to a time when we have also lost focus during a call," JT responded.

"Closing your eyes is one way to avoid getting distracted. As we've discussed, standing up is another, and a third option is to clear off your desk before the call starts. By removing clutter, you remove visual stimuli and make it far easier to focus on the discussion. If don't have time to clear, you can also determine a focal point that isn't distracting and keep your eyes there. Any of these tips will help you keep your head in the game. Anything else?" Heads shook around the room.

"Here's my question for you: Who in this room has participated in or led a conference call that when you hung up you thought, *Wow, that had real value, I'm glad I was on that call?*"

Fifty percent of the room raised their hands. "What was good about that call?" JT probed.

Ann immediately volunteered to share. "It was a collection point. In dealing with the merger, we created a collection point where both companies were on the call. It offered camaraderie and gave us a chance to ask, 'what have you learned this week?' It was really helpful because things were constantly changing. What I liked was the speed at which we traveled during that call. It's nice because we connected and then moved on."

JT responded, "Isn't it nice that you feel like there's value added in that call?"

Ann nodded affirmatively.

"Were you leading it or were you listening?" Al asked.

"I was leading it and I purposefully—because I don't know these people, I haven't met them—tried very hard to set up an agenda offering what I think, as well as asking them what they wanted to add to the call. I did this all beforehand to assure we were all considered equals and that everyone was involved. It worked out great."

"I host a call every week," David stated. "It's just a typical staff call with people I can't walk over and meet in person. One of the things that makes it really valuable is that I come prepared with an agenda and a goal of finishing within thirty minutes. I know who's on the line, offer introductions, and make sure all of the items are covered. It's a very, very structured call, and at the end, I always feel very good because I got all the points across, and I'm able to get feedback."

"You may not like coming to Massive because despite how Ann's doing things," Ron warned David, "most of the calls I'm on have no beginning and no end. There's no agenda, and it's very difficult to get anything out of them."

"I hear that a lot, Ron, and that's why I'm encouraged to hear both Ann and David say they do the same thing—prepare," JT said. "So my follow-up question to all of you is this: if you had a major presentation next Tuesday, would you spend more time preparing for a face-to-face or a conference call?"

"Face-to-face," they answered.

"I would, too; yet, guess what…the conference call is the harder of the two. But, we will spend more time preparing for that face-to-face because we are 'on'. Even so, I think the conference call is the harder of the two because you don't get the body language and you don't get the visual feedback to see how it's going. What do you see done wrong with your conference calls now?"

"Some of them are simply too long," Ajay answered. "It's just as Ron reported, there is no ending, and people are frequently repeating the information."

"Some of them are redundant," David said with a shrug.

"Some of them actually have no value whatsoever; it's just a conference call. It shouldn't even be held," Ron said, rolling his eyes.

"It's on the calendar, and therefore, we can never cancel. We must do it," Andrei responded.

"Or at some point in the past, someone decided we needed it, and now we just keep doing it. For all we know, that person has left the company," Laleh said, smiling. Laughter rang out.

"The complaints I hear over and over are: too long, no agenda, no purpose—why was I on the call?" JT told them.

"All right, let me share some other strategies that our clients have used to improve their conference calls. I don't think there's anything earth shattering on this list, but I do think we get so caught up in doing this daily that we forget to step back and think about some of the basics.

"I am convinced if you could improve these slightly, your brand will benefit significantly. Because how do most people feel about conference calls?" JT asked and then answered, "They have very negative feelings. Why? Because most people think conference calls are useless and a waste of time.

"So here goes:

- Include a POW

"I would still do the POW. After all, I still need to grab their attention in the first thirty to sixty seconds. One great way to start is to have an image that will visually surprise your audience.

- Include an Agenda Slide

"I am a firm believer if ever there was a place for an agenda slide, it's on a conference call. Even if it's been in the meeting invite. Sure, you've said it twelve times in an email, but I think it is still worth taking fifteen seconds to remind them about the three points of the conversation today. I also think fifteen seconds on the agenda reduces some interruptions.

"Let's say I didn't read your meeting invite; however, I see my topic of interest included in your agenda. Since I know you're going to cover it, I may not interrupt you.

"*If* you have the slide—great—you don't have to call it an agenda, and if you don't have it, I would at least verbally tell them 'this is what we're going to cover today.' It takes so little time and the pay off is great because you stay in control."

• Put the Agenda in a box on the Upper Right of Every Slide

"This one came from a Massive executive. Place the agenda in the upper box for calls longer than an hour. What is the longest length on some of these conference calls?"

"Three hours," Al answered.

"Every Friday," Ron groaned.

Andrei explained, "The issue is with the ones that are done everyday at certain times to discuss the operation. Those calls have no purpose—they're just saying what's going on. Those are three hours long, and they're the ones where you're not really sure if anyone is listening 'cause you know everyone is checking and sending emails."

Al added, "Not to mention, the three-hour Friday call is the same stuff every week. I might as well be looking at the presentation from two weeks ago."

"Isn't that scary?" JT asked. "Going back to the one POW suggestion—tell me something I don't know. Is there just one thing that's happened from last Friday to this Friday? If so, start with that. Do that incredibly well so that maybe, in some way out of that three-hour misery, you'll have become memorable.

"I liked this idea that came from Massive regarding those three-hour calls. Someone suggested putting a very small agenda box in the upper right-hand corner of every slide. They then highlight the font color to let you know what topic they're on because these calls are so long.

"So maybe the first slide could really be a POW and an agenda combo. For example, the slide could be a graphic ten million dollars written across the screen in big numbers because you're going to talk about a ten million dollar opportunity. On the bottom, you could put your three points, which is especially important on these three-hour calls.

- Change voices every 8-10 minutes

"To reiterate, even the best voices in the business know they can't hold an invisible audience for more than ten minutes. One of the best ways to manage this is to partner with someone for your presentation. If that's impossible, ask someone to call in at a specified time, so they can ask a question.

"One caution here is that you may want to avoid inviting questions if you don't have someone in the audience you know will be sure to participate," JT said with a shake of his head. "Q&A by phone can be difficult due to the timing. First, your audience has to realize they have a question. Then, it usually takes them a moment or two to get un-muted. As if that weren't enough of a gauntlet, they also have to avoid talking over someone else."

JT threw his hands in the air. "What do you do? Well, one great way to manage this is to instruct your audience to type in their questions. This allows them unfettered access to you without having to interrupt."

"Oh, they're not shy about interrupting," Ron said with a guffaw.

"I do understand that, Ron, but please keep in mind your executive presence is on display at all times, and leadership is comprised of small actions. Even an action as small as giving instructions on how to present questions during your meeting."

Ron could see the wisdom in trying JT's approach, particularly since he had no other ideas.

- A picture is worth a thousand words

"One of the challenges we face by having virtual meetings is missing the opportunity to connect in any visual way. A good 'connector,' you'll remember that term from our Minute to Win It exercise, is to exchange photos before you launch into business. These photos could include you, new team members, the outside of your building, a local landmark, etc. You get the idea. Building a brand is all about being memorable in positive ways. It's far easier for most people to remember an audio experience when it is combined with a visual.

- Insert Q&A between messages

"I had a client return to her agenda slide after each of her main messages. She would then ask for questions before moving on to her next topic. It provided great clarity regarding her three key points, as well as kept her audience clear on where they were in her program."

Ann was shaking her head, so JT asked her if she disagreed with the idea. "No, I don't disagree," she answered in very congenial tone. "I'm thinking about the number of meetings I go to that have no agenda and as many as fifty key points. I believe this type of organization could have an incredible impact, but I'm just wondering how we'll ever get people to change."

"Thank you for your comment, Ann. I certainly understand that this is a big ship to turn and bringing all of these techniques into daily practice isn't going to happen overnight. But, could I suggest that going forward, you see yourself as one who leads by example?"

Looking out at all of them, he added. "The proof of these techniques lies in the results you get from implementing them: shorter meetings, less need to repeat your agendas, higher levels of production, and therefore, satisfaction amongst your teams. Believe me, if your brand becomes known for interesting and efficient meeting leadership, they'll want to follow your example.

- 45 Minute Manager

"I can't tell you how often I hear clients tell me they're scheduled in back-to-back meetings from eight o'clock in the morning straight through until six o'clock or later. Without so much as a moment's break!"

"What's your point?" Ron sarcastically asked.

"So what happens by ten a.m.? That pace can't be maintained, so they start falling behind and end up showing up late to their meetings. The meeting leader then has to re-cap, which sets the meeting even further behind. Frankly, it's all a bit crazy.

"But, what if you could be the hero or heroine? What if you could give your colleagues an extra fifteen minutes to check email or grab a fresh cup of coffee? What if you gave them a chance to wrap up one meeting a few minutes late and then take a deep breath before showing up at your meeting on time? How? By starting your meetings at a quarter after the hour.

"Now, I know some of you might be thinking it would be hard to shorten your meetings. But, I invite you to really consider this idea. Because, when you apply the organizational tips we've discussed, I believe you'll find almost any meeting can be trimmed by fifteen minutes and still be effective. In fact, I'd be willing to bet your meetings will become even more effective from having a little less time. To tell you the truth, it adds focus for both you and your audience.

- Invite a guest speaker

"For those calls that are routine and don't have urgent business, you may want to introduce some variety into your agenda. One great way to stir things up is to invite someone from another department/division to speak briefly on a timely topic. Company newsletters and social media outlets are filled with people who like to tell people what they know. Seek out those around you who would welcome the chance to exchange information as well as network.

- Live studio audience

"If you're preparing for an important virtual meeting, do your best to get some people into a room with you during the call. Speaking in front of a live audience helps you keep up your energy, read the reaction of your audience as well as support you in maintaining your focus. As every entertainer will tell you, it's scarier to perform live, but you'll never dose off."

"Really?" Al asked. "You'd intentionally bring in an audience even if you don't have to?"

"Yes, Al," JT answered. "Because you're too strong as a leader to miss an opportunity to shine. Having those people in the room will strengthen every part of your delivery—your voice, your passion, and your focus. I promise you it will be worth it because your executive presence will not go unnoticed.

- Invite Follow-up

"Be sure you leave everyone with a clear understanding of what's next or at least how they can follow up. Accountability is the best way to facilitate progress.

- Automated participation

"There are many ways available through WebEx, Live Meeting, Outlook, and other programs to make your calls easier to access and more engaging. Through these programs, you can call a participant's phone automatically, create an on-line voting process where callers cast a vote for a strategy at the end of the virtual discussion, use your computer screen as a live white board, set-up up the video option so others on the call can actually see you, etc. The technology changes constantly so make sure you know what all your web meeting programs offer.

"Let's say five of you are on my call at ten a.m. This is an important call, and the group is in multiple locations. Did you know that if I asked for the phone number where you'll be on Friday at ten a.m., I can enter it in, and Friday morning at ten, your phone will ring, and you'll be on the call? You will not dial in, nor will you add a passcode; you'll simply be on the call."

"Really?" They asked in unison.

"Some of my friends at GE do this when they have a small number of participants on important calls, and people are traveling. You don't have to do anything except be sure to tell them it's going to happen. Otherwise, they may see a number they don't recognize and then not answer. For this one, the meeting organizer would pre-populate this with the relevant numbers and program it in.

"For larger meetings, you can include the toll free number and the passcode in the invitation, thus allowing attendees to tap the link and be taken directly into the call. Think about all the people traveling. Wouldn't it be nice for them to only have to tap the number?

- Non-verbal interaction

"Can you draw something on your screen? Visually, if someone is multitasking, and they see something moving on the screen, they'll look to see what's being discussed. The bottom is line is this—do all you can to engage your audiences because in the end, communication is about people connecting to people."

Act 9: Scene III

IMPACTFUL EMAILS

"Unfortunately, I regularly have eight hours of straight meetings," Laleh said with a sigh. "It's way too many conference calls, and the feedback I hear is 'we don't see you as much anymore.' I used to really enjoy getting to go out and connect."

JT nodded sympathetically. "Your story reminds me of another client who found herself getting disconnected. In her case, she was evaluated negatively for not reaching out to her team often enough, as well as not responding quickly to emails. After that review, she booked an hour every day to answer emails and then left her office so she could touch base with people. She found if she didn't block that hour in her calendar, someone would fill it."

"The bottom line is our employees and our direct reports are our customers," Al said. "And we don't always take care of our direct customers by being out there on the floor and just plain talking to the folks—interacting. We've lost so much of that over the years due to meetings and having to put together PowerPoint decks. We just don't have time to connect. It's sad because you can head off a lot more stuff or be far more proactive with things when you're out there dealing with the people. As you know."

Ann joined the conversation by admitting, "One of my directs once said I never ask him how he's doing. I can see how I have a habit of seeking out information without taking any time for a human connection."

"I get in a hurry to just get through stuff. I often just whip off an answer in an email and then they take it the wrong way," Ron commiserated.

"That's because we're technical people. We constantly hear comments that technical people 'talk down' to non-technical people," Andrei stated, annoyed at the criticism he'd received.

Laleh, as one of the few non-technical people in the room, jumped in, changing the direction of the conversation. "I'm the send-an-email-and-say 'hi, how are you doing?' type. That's just who I am. You should all know that I actually value the people who send a three-line email back. It doesn't rub me the wrong way. I don't mind receiving that type of communication even if I answer with a long email," she said reassuringly.

"Those of us who are technical know that nobody will get offended if we write back just what you're asking. That's all we want, the technical information. Once it goes outside of our department, you either have to dummy it up or put all the social stuff into it. I couldn't care less about all the social stuff. I just want the results. Then, they get all bent out of shape and say, 'I don't like the tone of your email.' I think it's time for some of these imbeciles to get some thicker skin and move on," Andrei reiterated.

"Exactly," Al agreed.

"I have a job to do," Ann stated matter-of-factly.

"I get the same feedback—with the 'tone,'" Ron said.

Interrupting what was about to become a classic gripe session, JT said. "When it's the back and forth, it's fine, but what happens when someone forwards it? Therein lies our issue."

"It's fine until some fool hits reply all," Ron said, rolling his eyes.

"Let's run through some basics for improving email communication.

- POW your subject line

"The typical manager receives two hundred to two hundred fifty emails a day at most of the companies where my consultants and I work," JT said with a shake of his head. "In order to be sure your emails stand out, you need an attention-grabbing subject line. The best way to do this is to write out your three key messages, then write your email, and finish up by crafting a POW.

- $C = A + B = C$

"The same rules apply to an effective email as they do to an effective presentation agenda. Be interesting right up front—find the most compelling point of your three and lead with it. The Tolstoy's of emails rarely get opened a third time.

- Edit, then edit, then edit again

"You never know where your words will end up. Editing will not only help you improve your writing, but it will also help you get your message streamlined. The old adage, 'less is more,' is absolutely true. So please, before you hit send, *please* edit yourself several times (especially on the really important emails) and *always* use spellcheck."

"One last note for those who have become really comfortable with texting, grammar still counts. Decision-makers are often people over fifty, and they will expect you to use appropriate grammar. Why? Because they've had to use it their entire lives, and they want you to suffer like they did.

- Reward/Reprimand Live

"Please do your best to reward someone face-to-face. Even if it's through Skype, great work deserves the time it takes to give someone a smile along with your appreciation. You may choose to send out an email announcing the win to the rest of your team, but first see how you might connect.

"I would caution you from ever reprimanding through an email. The possibilities for having a misunderstanding are far too great to make this reasonable. Furthermore, the chance of it being seen by others makes it much too risky.

- The Rule of Three

"At Black Sheep, we have a rule. If you've exchanged three emails on the same topic, and you have not yet clarified the situation—then it's time *to pick up the phone*," JT said emphatically. "As I said before, I have gotten swept up in threads of twenty emails just so I can schedule a conference call," JT rolled his eyes. "Please think about the value of making a call to work things out.

"As you can see, none of these ideas are huge, but all of them offer small ways to have a big impact on your email presence. Wouldn't it be wonderful to know that your emails are known for their clarity, brevity, and relevance? That would be quite a marketable brand."

Act 10: Scene I

TAKING SIDES (OF THE ROOM)

Question 8
If you are delivering a stand-up PowerPoint presentation, by which side of the projection screen should you stand for the majority of the presentation?

> *a. The audience's left side of the screen*
> *b. The audience's right side of the screen*

"Same side you're on," Ajay said.

"Okay, I tried to give you an answer," JT said, as he pointed to where he was standing. "Why would I rather you be here?"

"Because you read from left to right," Mizuki said quietly. "Say it again, Mizuki."

"You read from left to right."

"Thank you. In most countries and cultures, people read and look from left to right."

If you are over here," JT moved to the right of the screen, "what will your audience look at first?"

"The screen," Mizuki answered.

"Then who became the star of your show? Not you. A PowerPoint slide did. Please don't ever get on this side of the room. It's okay to move with purpose, and if you come over here for a slide or two, fine. But for the majority of the time, you stay in your anchor position over on the left so they look to you first and then go to the slide second."

"The podiums I've had to work with were all screwed into the floor and the microphone was attached to it," Ron stated. "What do you do then?"

"Unfortunately, we all have to work with the room we're given, don't we?" JT asked with a sigh. "And sometimes, we have no choice. I tell you, whenever I see that set up at a conference, I just cringe because it makes it so much harder for the speaker to connect to the audience. Frankly, I believe it's a reflection of our business culture that supports leaders in handing over their power to slides."

- Microphones

"Speaking of microphones, who's had to use audio in their presentations?" Most of them raised their hands. "Let's take two minutes and talk about microphones. Pretend this dry-erase marker is a microphone, and now pretend you are now walking up to do your presentation.

"This is something I better never see you do, because it makes me hear, 'Priority Access, now boarding,'" he warned.

Blowing and tapping the marker, he said. "Is this thing on? Can you hear me? If you have ever blown on or tapped into a microphone, please don't ever do it again. It detracts from your executive presence and is simply not the sign of a professional. As the speaker, you should have already checked out your sound, so you know it's right. Do it before people get in the room.

"As for the microphones on a stick or a stand, what do you do when you have no choice but to use it?" Raising his marker out in front of his body, he continued, "Pretend this microphone is attached to a podium. This is what I see people do," JT leaned forward. 'Thank you all so much for coming today….'

"Please do not ever lean into a microphone. Here's what you need to do. Walk up and adjust the mic, so it will stand under your chin. This will give you good audio, as well as allow the audience to see your facial expressions."

"What if the microphone's dead? 'Cause sometimes you can't tell, and then they yell, 'we can't hear you,'" Al inquired.

"I would use humor. For example:

I realize this is not on. Ron, really, you think I'm so bad that you killed the microphone? You took out the battery, didn't you, Ron?

"I'd make fun of it somehow. Certainly somebody who's close by will get you a good microphone, but I think the best thing that you can ever use is a clip-on lavaliere. It will let you be natural, and it will allow you to use your hands and arms appropriately.

"However, I would prefer not to see a cord running down the front of your shirt or blouse. It doesn't look neat. You need to think about what you're wearing that day, so you can hook the box in back and run the cord under your clothes."

"What if you really suck at the hand gestures? Can a handheld microphone be your saving grace?" Ron quasi-jested.

"It could be provided you're not…." JT demonstrated a very stiff body with a frozen expression and a shaky hand. "Though I have to say, I always vote for a clip-on lavaliere."

Act 10: Scene II

PROFESSIONAL APPEARANCE

"Projecting a professional appearance. How important is it to your executive brand?" JT posed. He received head nods in response from the women; however, the men in the group didn't seem concerned about the importance of appearance.

"I'm not about to tell you what you should or should not wear, but I will give you a quick story because I know this is very important.

"A seasoned manager at a large international corporation called me after one of my programs and thanked me for helping the group with their executive presence. This person was one of the standouts in the group...both good and not so good. She said, 'JT I want you to be honest with me, I feel like you were holding back around professional appearance and there was something you wanted to tell me.'

"I said, 'Okay, you called me, so I'm going to be honest with you.' I told her what a great communicator she was. Honestly, she was the best presenter in her program. I said, 'Here's what I need to tell you: You need to modernize your appearance. Your clothes, your hairstyle, and your glasses look dated.'

"When someone looks dated, what's the perception others could have of them?" JT asked and then responded, "Others may think they're not relevant, that the person is stuck in a time warp, unwilling to embrace new ideas, and possibly afraid of new technology. Regardless of whether or not it's true, that will be the perception and so much of executive presence is based on perception.

"In today's world, you have to appear modern in style and appearance. That doesn't mean you have to be fashion forward, but it does mean you cannot have a 'dated' appearance."

"Here are my points about professional appearance. Whoever your audience is, whatever your meeting is, if you're presenting that day, I encourage people to do the following:

- Dress Plus One Up from your Audience

"Bear in mind I said plus one, not three. There is nothing wrong with being slightly above most of the people in that audience. You know who the audience is on that given day, and therefore, what will work. It may be the difference of wearing or not wearing a jacket. Or it might be the difference between a long-sleeved or a short-sleeved shirt."

"So if they're all wearing suits, do we need to put on a tuxedo?" Ron inquired.

"Yes, yes, Ron. I encourage you to wear a tux to the next board meeting. To the rest of you, I will need someone to take pictures of that event for me."

- Fit is More Important than Cost

"You do not have to spend a lot of money on clothes. The biggest struggle I see people face is clothes that do not properly fit. Nobody does discount shopping better than me. But you need to spend a few extra dollars to make everything fit well. When your clothes fit well, you just look very polished and put together."

- Try it on in the store

"I know you, Ron," JT teased. "I know you're the kind of guy who won't try something on, you'll just buy it. Then you get it home and discover it isn't a great fit, but you hang it up in the closet anyway because you don't like returning things. Then comes the morning when the laundry has fallen off and *bang*, suddenly that ill-fitting shirt isn't so bad." Shaking his head, JT cautioned, "Just say no, Ron. Because I can assure you, the shirt has not magically improved by hanging in the closet. Just say no, and next time try it on before you get it home."

- Social Settings

"Who likes to network?" JT asked the group. No one raised a hand. Ron looked over to Laleh, "Come on now, don't be shy."

"I see why you might think I enjoy it because I'm comfortable with public speaking. But to be honest, I find networking to be just that, 'work' and most of the time, I'd much rather be doing almost anything else."

JT nodded, "You know, in the fifteen years since I started doing this program, I've only had a few people raise their hands to that question. So, the first thing you need to remember is that you're not alone. The next time you walk into a room filled with strangers, remind yourself that they are almost all of them are just as miserable as you are. That should help you feel at least a little bit better.

"The next thing you want to do is get a glass in your hand. I'm not suggesting that you sprint to the bar, but I do recommend that you head in that direction first. Having a drink in your hand automatically tells people you're planning on staying at least long enough to have a conversation."

"Does it need to have alcohol to be acceptable?" Ajay inquired.

"No," JT assured him. "Juice, a soft drink, or water is fine. You just want to have something that makes you look like you belong. Of course, you'll want to carry it in your left hand. Why is that?"

"So you can shake hands," David responded.

"Right, so you can offer someone a warm, dry hand to shake," JT affirmed.

"People struggle in cocktail settings or at social events to know which topics are appropriate for conversation. What do you need to avoid?"

"Politics, religion…and well, yes, politics and religion," Ann said.

"And I would add questions that are too personal to that list," JT inserted.

"Here are a couple of inappropriate questions I see people ask when they are first meeting someone, 'Are you married?' or 'Do you have children?' Imagine if that person was freshly divorced, and you've just brought up a painful experience for them. What you could say is, 'Tell me about your family.' That is a very different tack that allows them to divulge information within their comfort zones. Of course, if they bring the family up in the conversation, then you can respond back. But, I would know something about a current event that's not controversial, or maybe something about the person's background that could help you carry on a conversation. I would always avoid politics, religion, and questions that are too personal."

During their next break, Al walked over to JT and asked for a private conversation. "Walking into this room, I was feeling too old to deal with this merger and all of the changes. But after all we've talked about, I'm wondering if I might be headed off to pasture a bit too soon. What do you think?"

"Well, Al," JT answered, looking him in the eye. "I can tell you this, unless you have something wonderful planned for your retirement, I think it would be a huge loss for everyone if you left." Al smiled and dropped his eyes to the floor. "You have invaluable experience, as well as the foundation to be a powerful speaker. Let me ask you this, what's your dream job?"

"Well, like I said, no one in my family has ever been a plant manager until me. So I kinda figured I'd reached the top. But now I'm wondering if I might be able to get a regional director-type of position. Until today, I never thought that was a possibility. Now...."

"Then let me be a true friend and tell you this: If you want to move up, it's time for you to buy new glasses and an updated wardrobe. The golf shirts and jeans that got you to your current position will keep you in that position. You'll need to see yourself as belonging in the new role, and therefore, dressing the part. In other words, it's time to create Al 2.0." They both laughed.

Al then scratched his head. "I'm an old bachelor at this point in my life, JT. I have no idea where to start."

JT paused. Al was an all-around good guy who had a rational dream. JT also knew Al wasn't going to get there on his own. "Al, I'm about to extend an invitation to you that I have never extended in all of my career." He shook his head in disbelief at what he was about to say, and Al began to look concerned.

"Al, I'm going to take you shopping," JT announced, clapping Al on the shoulder. "So get your credit card and be ready to hit the ground running right after we finish up today." Though he was going to be pressed for time, JT also knew it would be crucial to help Al while he was still feeling ready for change.

"Can't say I saw this coming," Al said with a chuckle. "I hope we don't run into anyone I know…."

"Me too, Al." JT said with a laugh.

Act 11: Scene I

DISTRACTED DECISION-MAKERS

Question 9
If a key stakeholder has become disengaged (gets on their
phone) in a meeting, you should ignore the person and
focus on those who seem interested.

a. True
b. False

"False," they answered.

"False," JT affirmed. "The answer is false, but how do you re-engage people?

"Let's say David is a key stakeholder and just as I am about to make a critical point, I see him doing this." JT pulled out his phone and appeared to be checking emails. "How might I re-engage David as a key stakeholder?"

"Cattle prod?" Ron suggested.

"With a black sheep brand!" JT embellished. "Okay, really, what might I do to re-engage him?"

"Nothing," Ajay suggested.

"Ask him a question," Ann offered.

"That's true, Ann. My natural response is to address him. However, I would highly recommend you avoid that tactic. Frankly, I say don't ever ask him a direct question," JT warned.

"As you're stating something or addressing it on a slide, use his name," Laleh suggested.

"That I'll give you, Laleh. But I would never say, 'So David, could you share your perspective on…?' Because it looks like you're calling out the student for bad behavior, and he is the senior leader. I wouldn't do that for anything in the world. But there are ways you can re-engage.

"Number one: If it's a two-hour meeting maybe it's time for a five-minute break. But let's say it's not a two-hour gathering, and you don't have the time. If you are physically standing, what could you do?" JT began casually walking toward David. "You could move slightly closer to the disengaged party.

"Both your presence and your volume may get him to raise his head, as well as the fact that he knows all eyes are following you. Therefore, if you're standing near him, all eyes will be on him.

"Now, obviously you can't go up to him like this," JT said, aggressively walking toward David. "Though I'd like to go up to him like this." JT mimed walking with his hands out as though he'd choke David. "Just keep it casual, like you really haven't thought about it." While he spoke, JT strolled over by David without ever looking directly at him.

"Another way to get attention is through something you say:

The next point I am going to share with you today will drive our decision. There's no doubt in my mind, so let me draw your attention as we look at our growth projection."

JT pointed at the slide behind him as though emphasizing his point. "You have to make it say something," he said, snapping his fingers.

"So you're emphasizing a point?" Ron asked.

"That you're about to make a major point that's critical to life," JT clarified. "You could also move to the screen. Movement might pull him back in.

"Here's what I see work the best:

The next point I want to make today is really critical to our decision. Al, [Al was seated next to David] do you mind sharing with the team what happened yesterday when you were on the conference call with the CEO? That really sets the stage for what we're going to talk about now.

"Tell them what happened yesterday. Get someone near the culprit talking with an easy, relevant, relatable question. Give them something he or she can answer in a minute or less. When you can get someone near the culprit talking, you have a much better chance of bringing them back in."

"Would it have to be someone on your own team?" Ron asked.

"Yes," answered JT. "You have to make it work. It can only work if...."

"You don't want to hand over control, right?" Ann interrupted.

"Yes, only if it works, make sense, and you know they can do it quickly."

Ron added, "It does catch the person off-guard. It would have to be a short answer."

"Absolutely," JT agreed. "This assumes you and I have had that other conversation, and therefore, I am confident that you can do that and do it well.

"To Ann's point, could you use David's name? Maybe, but you have to be a very good actor or actress to pull it off. If you *can* pull it off, it should look something like this:

> You know the next point I'm going to make is really critical to our decision. I had the chance to talk with David this morning before the meeting, and he shared with me his perspective that this solution has the potential to work.

"Did I look at him when I said his name?" JT emphatically shook his head. "*No*, don't you even think about looking over at David while you're saying something like this."

"And it was something you said," Al added. "You said his solution could work."

"That's right. You can bring him in that way, but you'd better be very good at it. And whatever you do, don't dart your eyes over there to David. Never call out the student for bad behavior.

"So what happens if David leaves the room?" JT asked. "There's no need to go on right?" David questioned.

"I think you have a couple of strategies. If it's a two-hour meeting, then give everyone five minutes:

> May we take a five-minute break at this point? It's going to be critical for us to share our next perspective with David.

"I would do that. Or let's say you can't go on, but for some reason, you can't send them out for fear that you'll never get them back. I've also seen this work very well:

I want to make the next critical point, and we're going to need David to be able to share his perspective on it. However, I'd like to stop where we are right now to get your thoughts on where you see our next actions after what you've heard so far. What do you think are some key strategies we need to implement going forward?

"Get them talking about the topic with something that's not too hard."

Act 11: Scene II

STORYTELLING

"To have a truly memorable impact, I cannot emphasize enough the power of a good story," JT stated emphatically. "In today's marketplace, eighty data points on the slide is no longer enough to sell your message, your project, or your proposal. Storytelling is trending with companies all over the world. In fact, classes on how to craft and deliver a good story are now being offered at ivy-league universities.

"If I needed any evidence of the trend, it came last year when we got a call from a Fortune 500 company to participate in an RFP for a two-day program on storytelling. They said, 'Don't bring in presentation skills. We aren't looking for that. What we need is good storytelling because that's what we think it takes to be influential.'

"It was a real wake up for my team. It spoke volumes to us about the power that companies place on that. Here's this major corporation saying 'we don't care about PowerPoint; we care about how these people tell stories because we're convinced that's how you influence people to move them into action.'

"For example, several years ago, there was a best-selling book on leading change. It was a good book all about how you bring change into an organization and affect the dynamic. In its heyday, it sold two million copies—a very respectable number. A second author wrote a book about how individuals respond to change. However, the second author presented his theories in a story, fable format. How many copies do you guess that author sold?"

"Five-hundred thousand," guessed Ron.

"One million," answered Ann.

"Five million," Laleh offered, much to the amusement of the others.

"More than twenty-six million copies." JT informed the stunned group.

"Yes, you do have to present facts and statistics, but what is memorable? The story. Storytelling is a big part of executive presence. You influence people through powerful stories.

"Let me be clear, a story can be very quick. It can be an example, like this:

Ron, do you remember our meeting with the government rep on Monday? I thought what she said to us was really powerful. Do you remember when she said...?

"That's a story. Because I took you out of this room, and I took you out of PowerPoint, and I took you somewhere else. I gave you characters and results and made you care about them. I gave you suspense.

"Who comes to mind as good storytellers at either Massive or Cascade?"

A lone seagull cry was the only response.

"One of my maintenance mechanics," Al finally answered. "I could listen to that whole crew everyday. You can't make this stuff up."

"I don't hear a lot of stories," Ann said.

"Then opportunity is knocking. If you can't think of a good storyteller, the time is now for one of you to step up. People will remember your story, and you, three days later and ten days later.

"Sharing stories forces us to focus on the words that we use and the impact they have. One of our consultants loves to show a particular video of a man out on the street. He's blind. He has a sign that says 'Help the Blind,' and people walk by and hardly throw anything into the hat he has sitting in front of him.

"Then this woman walks up, and she takes his sign and flips it over. She writes something on it, and of course, we can't see the words, but suddenly the money starts flowing in. At the end, they show what she's written, 'It's a beautiful day, and I can't see it.' It's very powerful."

"I've seen that," Ann said. "I agree. It is really powerful."

"You have to be good storytellers. It's part of what we do," JT stated. "As I said, stories can be very short. In fact, they can be six words or less." That caught them off guard, as it did every audience.

"It is said that Hemingway was asked to write the shortest possible novel. He wrote, 'For sale: Baby shoes, never worn.'" JT paused to let them absorb the power of the story. "'For sale: Baby shoes, never worn.' Six words that tell a compelling story.

"The concept of putting our stories into six words took off. Today there is a SixWordMemoirs.com website, there are published collections of six word stories, and the exercise of writing a six-word story is included in the curriculum at the Stanford School of Business.

"We've seen some great ones through this program:

Golden retriever trapped in a human body.
Lots of kids. Extra wide hips.

Middle child. Learned to negotiate.
Travel—seventy-eight countries and counting.

"As you can see, there are no rules to this. The goal is to simply get quiet for a minute and see what six words float to the top. If you end up writing four words, or even ten, that's fine, too. We're just looking to practice writing a very short story. So, please, take the next few minutes to write your own six word memoir."

JT could see that Ann was struggling. "What are you passionate about?" He asked quietly.

"I don't know. Really all I do is work," Ann answered.

Ron rolled his eyes and said, "Ann, all you and your partner ever talk about is cars."

A smile crept across her face, but then quickly faded. "Yes, but that's where the trouble started…." Ann sunk into her memory, her face twisting first into grief then brightening with awareness.

"Okay, I've got this," she said. JT walked away. Ron returned to his own story.

Laleh volunteered to be the first to share. Speaking in almost a whisper, she said, "I'm waiting for your eyes to open."

Bringing her voice back to a normal volume, she explained. "Last year my husband was in a car crash that put him in a coma. For three days, I sat by his bedside waiting and watching for his eyes to open." She paused. "I'm not sure why, but I was absolutely convinced if I could just see his eyes, even if it was through a drugged haze—everything would be okay. So for three days, the only thought I had was *I'm waiting for your eyes to open…I'm waiting for your eyes to open…I'm waiting for your eyes to open*…and then they did."

After taking a deep breath, she added. "That accident was one year ago today." She shook her head. "I can't believe it was only a year ago, nor can I believe it wasn't yesterday. I'm glad we're doing this exercise because…," she choked up for just a moment, "…I just want to remember how lucky I am."

As though on cue, the large wind chimes on the porch rang out—like bells—in celebration.

Figuring he may as well get it over with, Ron volunteered to share next. "Mind of its own, damn lawnmower." He smiled. "I know it's not terribly deep." He turned to sit down, then hesitated. "I have another one. Would you like me to share that too?"

"By all means," JT replied.

Ron stepped back to the front. "Can't write. Can't read. Must talk." Though Ron had expected a laugh, he was met with compassionate silence. Suddenly he was embarrassed. "I'm…ah…I'm dyslexic. So, I talk any chance I get."

"I've seen your written reports, Ron," David offered. "And I had no idea."

Ron nodded, "I have an incredible assistant who keeps me from looking like a poorly educated third grader."

"It's good it hasn't kept you from success," Mizuki observed.

"I still try to hide it," Ron confessed. "I wasn't sure I should say anything…." He shrugged. "Oh well, too late now."

"I trust we're all professionals here, Ron," JT reassured him. "While I certainly don't see any reason for you to feel shame, I'm also confident your story is safe in our care." Everyone agreed.

"Thanks," Ron replied softly. He'd never been this vulnerable in front of anyone, much less his peers. To do so twice in one day had to mean something profound was shifting for him. He returned to his seat, thoughtful and introspective—two words that rarely described him.

Ann went next. "The sound of the horses died." She sighed. "For twenty years, I owned a gorgeous, cherry red Ford Mustang with a black convertible top." Ann needed an extra breath. "She never had a scratch on her until someone I love left her out one night, and…my baby…

was totaled by a passing car. I realize in light of Laleh's story this may seem trivial, but for me, it was devastating. So much so, that I'm pretty sure I've been grieving ever since. Funny, I hadn't thought about it until doing this."

"Me too, Ann," Laleh agreed. "I was really surprised by the six words that came up."

"That's what I love about doing this exercise," JT said. "It allows us to hear what's on our own minds."

"The other aspect of this that I really appreciate is how much we get to know about each other in a very short period of time. If you ever need a team builder, this is a good one."

"Every leader has unique experiences that provide rich learning opportunities for others. Taking the time to craft a personal narrative that reflects your style and leadership perspective is a really effective way to strengthen your professional brand.

"What I'd like you to do now is write a three-to-five-minute 'Signature Narrative' that you'll be delivering to the group."

A slide popped up on the screen:

1. *How did you get involved in manufacturing?*
2. *How did you arrive at Massive/Cascade?*
3. *What is your current connection to Massive/Cascade?*
4. *What is your personal mission statement?*

"You can spend a few minutes answering one of these questions or take it in a completely different direction. The key here is to tell us who you are as a leader, how leadership affects your life, and where you want to go."

David volunteered to present first. "Growing up, my dad used to beat the crap out of me. It wasn't just me—he pounded on my brothers, too. As much as we hated getting hit, my brothers and I would take down anyone that bad-mouthed my old man. When I came to Cascade as a scrappy kid, I didn't know anything about leadership. But I knew the value of loyalty first-hand.

"As this merger has progressed, the one thing I've said to my people is that I would defend them as much as humanly possible. I've been told more than once that I should have jumped ship long ago because the *real* opportunities are going to be saved for people like Andrei." David shrugged with resign.

"Now that I've met Andrei, I can see they were right. From a career perspective, I should have bailed. But for as much as my dad was a tried-and-true SOB—pardon my language—he always said you never leave a man behind. And I guess, the one thing worse than not knowing what's next would be to have people say I abandoned my team when things got tough." Not waiting for a response, David walked back to his seat.

JT let everyone absorb the moment, and for the first time in hours, he noticed the sound of the surf. He assumed that meant the tide had come in.

Several of them stole glances over at Andrei, trying to read his face. They knew he'd been spoiling for a fight with David all day, and they couldn't help but wonder if he was now preparing to go in for the kill.

Andrei slowly rose and made his way to the front of the room. "David," he said with a level of respect they'd not heard before, "I, too, grew up in a culture of battle. We didn't see competition as a game; it was a matter of survival. The last man standing assumed leadership, and yes, I was always the last one standing. What some of you see as arrogance was necessary to keep my family, my neighbors, and eventually my platoon, alive."

Addressing JT, he said, "You ask about my leadership style, but I don't think about these things. When I lead, I don't contemplate the orders I give or think about the way I say them. I just lead and expect everyone to follow. Anything less is intolerable and likely to get you killed."

Andrei looked back to the group. "I walked into this house to go to war with David. I considered him the greatest challenge for my position, and I was right. He is. But this battle is not what I thought it would be.

"David, you are the leader I will never be happy being. You are a product of a democracy. You lead by building teams, delivering inspirational speeches, and making decisions by committee. I am a product of a dictatorship. I lead by rank and power. We are both useful to our troops, but only when we are in the correct environment."

Again turning to JT, he said, "You laid out a model of the modern western leader. I agree your model is valid. Your presence here says that Massive also believes in your model of leadership. The problem for me is that the marketplace you keep referencing is one in which I do not fit.

"This is not the first time I have felt like an outsider. Each time I have a job review, I hear the same thing—I must change how I behave and therefore, how I think. But the truth is, I don't choose to change. I am who I am, and I have no interest in becoming some westernized version of myself that I don't recognize in the mirror.

"I have given this much thought, and today's session has confirmed it. I don't belong. Therefore, I am going to return to my native land and re-join the military where my leadership is valued and respected."

For the second time that day, Andrei had delivered a message that left the room in stunned silence. "Now that I have made my decision, I am far too restless to stay and finish this program. I am going to leave now and begin my extraction from Massive. It has been fascinating to spend this day together. Thank you."

Andrei gathered his belongings and shook their hands one-by-one before exiting the room.

Act 12: Scene I

THE IMPORTANCE OF TIMING

"Speaking of timing...." JT said to the group after they'd recuperated from Andrei's rapid departure.

Question 10
When you tell the audience you are about
to conclude, you should do so within:
a. Sixty seconds
b. Three minutes
c. Ten seconds

"A, B, or C? Which did you say it was?" JT asked. He heard all three answers. The red circle appeared around the A. "It can be thirty to forty-five seconds." He told them. "Ten seconds is too fast, and three minutes is too long. When people hear, 'in conclusion' they mentally start doing what?"

"Packing," Ron answered.

"Yes, they start winding down," JT agreed. "There are three components of a good conclusion. I rarely see people do this, but I assure you, you will look like a great leader with executive presence if you risk being the exception:

1. A reminder of your three key messages.

"Very quickly, this is not a full explanation, just a quick reminder. A great way to do it is to use the Q&A slide.

2. A call to action.

"What are these people supposed to do when they walk out of the room? Do you go to presentations and meetings and say, 'Why was I there?' Of course you do. I blame part of that on the speaker because they weren't clear about their call to action.

3. End with some strong sentences. Start strong and end strong, don't let it go flat in the last ten seconds.

"For example:

Before we leave this room today, I want to take a moment to thank you. I owe all of you a debt of gratitude. I never anticipated that this project we were assigned would take the team this long to do. We did it, and we did it incredibly well. Please know how grateful I am. I'll see you next Tuesday in our staff meeting. Have a great week.

"End strong. Maintain your command right up to the end.

"All right, there were ten questions on the quiz. Let's see who gets the prize. Remember, I gave you number five for free no matter what you answered. Please count up how many you got."

"I got them all," Laleh said in a soft voice, not wanting to sound as proud as she felt.

"Laleh, you got them all right?" JT asked with surprise. "That's a Black Sheep first! Did anyone else get them all?" No one else did.

"Well, Laleh, congratulations because you are going to get the lottery prize. Now Laleh, I know you'd like a lottery ticket, or you'd like me to channel you tonight's winning Powerball numbers. But I have something much more valuable than the winning numbers or the Powerball millions for you. From the lottery television show, we have the official JT photo just for you." JT held up his publicity shot complete with an autograph.

The group erupted into a loud cackle of hoots and hollers. Laleh put her hand over her heart as she accepted her "prize."

"If that doesn't prove that I am shallow and superficial...what's it going to take here, people?"

The gang launched into a discussion regarding the perfect location for the new treasure.

When they'd settled down a bit, JT said, "All right, tell me something you're going to take from that quiz. Just share something that really resonated with you that will give you a different perspective on how you think about your communications and presentations."

"Some of the things that we did in the past, the things that we were taught how to do were incorrect," Al answered. "Because most of us have 'PowerPoint-ed' our way through our careers, and we were told this is how you do certain things. Everyone just took the corporate one and copied it. We didn't know we were putting the wrong stuff on it."

"I love that comment: We were 'PowerPoint-ed' through our careers. That's a great line. Thank you, what else?"

"I love the pausing with the black screen," Ann said.

"That's something. You think you know a program on the computer, and then you learn something like this, and you realize how much you don't know," Ron added.

"I love training. I find the whole process of learning new things exciting," Laleh began. "However, to be honest, I wasn't sure this program was going to have much to teach me. I've been pretty comfortable giving presentations for as long as I can remember, so I doubted today would provide any new and valuable information. I have to say I couldn't have been more wrong." She smiled over at JT. "Thanks to you and your program, I learned all sorts of priceless tips and techniques. It's been great.

"However, my biggest take-away came from sharing this day with all of you." She paused. "My days at Massive have become focused on the endless race to discover new training methodologies and technologies and doing everything possible to recruit the best and the brightest. The pace has become so fast, it has eliminated the time for human connections."

Looking at each of them she continued, "Being here today has reminded me how much I'm missing by not taking the time to nurture the resources we already have at Massive: your leadership, your passion, your experience, your knowledge, and your loyalty. Not to mention all of the wonderful ideas and visions of our post-merger company that you've shared with me during the breaks.

"Going forward, I want to dedicate much of my time to helping our new blended team find their voices and hone their communication skills, so we don't lose their contributions in a sea of change. It's funny, I came today thinking I'd learn about communication, never considering I'd transform as a leader. Thank you all."

"JT?" Mizuki raised her hand. "I have learned many things today especially about how we need to practice telling our story. You mentioned I might have another chance to introduce myself. May I do that now?"

"Certainly," JT replied as he gave her the floor.

"My name is Mizuki, and I have no business being in this room. Unlike all of you, I am new to the company and this is my first job. I have never been in management. In fact, I am still taking college courses at night.

"I am here because someone very high up in the company told me to be here and spy on all of you. I promise you, it was not Tom or Kelly." They gasped at hearing this young, seemingly innocent woman reveal such deception.

"These notes I have been taking were all about what's been happening here. I was told to observe you all and then put together a report of everything I've seen so it can be used to…," she stammered, "…used to see who gets fired. If the person who ordered me to do this had been the CEO, I would tell each of you to run for your souls. However, please know this is not the case. The CEO strikes me as a very wise man, and I don't believe he has any knowledge of this."

"The person expecting this report belongs is not the kind of leader you all deserve to have. Therefore, it is my intention to reveal this man to my superiors, so those in authority may determine his fate.

"With your permission, I'd like to read to you my report for today."

There was no precedent for this, but JT had a gut feeling it was going to be okay. "Proceed."

"Thank you. Executive Presence Training—Final Report on Participants:

"This training session has provided life-changing opportunities for the attendees and each of them has stepped up to the challenges given them. It has been my honor to watch a heart soften with forgiveness," she paused to give Ann a tender look. "I have seen a lion make the decision to roar once more." She smiled at Al. "I saw a wounded warrior re-claim his sword," she added, nodding to Ron. "I met a very kind soul," looking over to Ajay. "I watched a soldier return to his troops," reminding them all of Andrei's sudden departure. "And I witnessed first-hand how true leaders remain authentic," she acknowledged, bowing to David and Laleh.

Putting down her notes, she said, "I don't know if I'll ever see any of you again, but I do know I will never forget spending this day together. Thank you."

Turning to JT, she added. "Nor will I ever forget the day I learned to talk about myself for sixty seconds. Thank you."

"You are most welcome," JT answered.

"We'll all see you again, Mizuki. You're a part of the Massive family now." David stated, fully stepping into the role Andrei had vacated. "I'll see to it you're protected as you reveal the truth."

As one, they stood up to rally around her and each other, completely ignoring which logo they were wearing.[8]

---

8   To subscribe to the Black Sheep community, scan this
     QR code.

Epilogue

RAISING YOUR VISIBILITY

Dear Reader,

I am amazed at the number of executives I meet who have no marketing plan. I'm here to tell you it is not HR's responsibility, it is not your manager's responsibility, it is *your* responsibility to sell your brand—authentically. But to do so, you have to raise your visibility.

You can raise your visibility at any company. Maybe you volunteer for a project no one else wanted. Maybe it's a project that's a little out of your typical work area because you want other people to get to see you. Maybe it's a charitable event sponsored by the company. You have to be seen; you have to raise your visibility. I challenge you to think of four things—one per quarter—which you can do to raise your visibility. When you raise your visibility, you raise your executive presence.

You are the face and voice of your company. You are presented with opportunities to protect and promote your company's brand every day.

May you also never forget that you should always be working on your brand.

Jeffrey T. Black

ABOUT THE AUTHORS

 **Jeff Black** has had to tell his clients all kinds of not-so-nice things...all in the name of Executive Presence. "Your hairstyle went out of style–three decades ago." "Your communication skills need an extreme makeover." "It's time to take control and command of the room!" Yet, he does it in such an entertaining way that his clients keep coming back for more. The Black Sheep customer list includes: GE, American Airlines, Procter & Gamble, Lockheed Martin, US Army, Bank of America, NBC, Notre Dame and other large corporations, government, educational and non-profit organizations.

While professing not to have much "substance and depth," Jeff indeed has the knowledge and experience to help those get to the next level in their careers. His Executive Presence strategies were formulated during his work in television–both in front of and behind the camera as:

assistant to the executive producer of a primetime TV drama, weather anchor, news reporter, and on-air host for his state's lottery drawing.

Over the past twenty years and across twenty different countries, Jeff has been cajoling leaders up the ladder. From C-level executives to mid-level managers, to total strangers on the street, Jeff tells everyone, "It's your responsibility to build your brand and market yourself. Not your HR manager or your boss, yours. Now, go forth, and *Unleash your BS!*"

Carol Hamilton has been a storyteller her entire life—and many of them have even been true! She is a published poet as well as the author of *Changing Your Story* (a collection of stories about people who transformed their lives by changing their perspectives). Carol has taken her love of storytelling to TEDxGreenville, corporate keynotes, and as a guest on numerous television and radio talk shows.

As a Black Sheep facilitator, executive coach and senior communications consultant, Carol conducts private coaching sessions and interactive seminars with leaders from top organizations including: GE, Lockheed Martin, American Airlines, U.S. Army, Arrow Electronics, Clemson University, University of North Carolina, and many more.

Inspiring others to own their power propels **Kimberly Faith Madden** out of bed each morning as she travels from coast to coast and across the globe. It has been her privilege to train and coach over twelve thousand leaders from hundreds of corporations with leaders from eighteen countries spanning twelve industries. Known as an engaging speaker, facilitator, executive coach, and consultant, Kim brings experience that ranges from community building and entrepreneurship to leadership development, communication skills, systems thinking, and team building. Her easygoing style and sense of humor make her a hit with audiences large and small.

She understands the facets of corporate cultures and uses her facilitations skills to challenge people to step outside their comfort zones and stand out in a crowded marketplace. Kim has a wealth of experience working with diverse leadership groups such as Hispanic Forums, Asian-American Councils, and is especially known for her impactful work with women's groups. She has been featured in articles for *Women's Entrepreneurship Magazine, Ladies Who Launch,* and the *Wall Street Journal.* Kim was recently published in *Women's World Magazine.*

CPSIA information can be obtained at www.ICGtesting.com
Printed in the USA
BVOW02s0906040215

386351BV00003B/61/P

9 781630 473570